Star Paddleboarding 2.0

Top 101 Stand Up Paddle Board Tips, Tricks, and Terms to Have Fun, Get Fit, Enjoy Nature, and Live Your Stand-Up Paddle Boarding Passion to the Fullest From A to Z!

HowExpert with Kayla Anderson

For more tips related to this topic, visit www.HowExpert.com/paddleboard.

Recommended Resources

www.HowExpert.com – Quick 'How To' Guides on Unique Topics by Everyday Experts.

www.HowExpert.com/writers - Write About Your #1 Passion/Knowledge/Experience.

www.HowExpert.com/membership - Learn a New 'How To' Topic About Practically Everything Every Week.

www.HowExpert.com/jobs - Check Out HowExpert Jobs.

Table of Contents

Introduction

In the summer of 2017, I got a job at a café/paddleboard rental shop on the North Shore of Lake Tahoe called Waterman's Landing. It is a family-owned business that supports the sport of stand-up paddleboarding and healthy living. After working all summer and only paddleboarding a couple of times, I decided to enter my first SUP race. I created a training plan and dedicated a lot more time out on the water, working on improving my technique, strength, stamina, and endurance. In the process, I started to feel more balanced, connected with nature, and mindful of my surroundings. Not only did I lose weight, but I made friends in the paddling community, tapped into the resources I had available at Waterman's Landing, and came away from the water happier and healthier.

I wrote a HowExpert book about my experience titled ***Stand Up Paddle Board Racing for Beginners: A Quick Guide on Training for Your First Stand Up Paddleboarding Competition***. In that book, I share an in-depth look at how I got into paddleboarding and my personal experiences about training for a race.

It snowed all winter in Lake Tahoe and then as spring rolled around, I started jonesing to get back out on the water again. I started paddling several times a week and trying to remember what I had learned the previous season. This prompted me to want to write another book about every term I've ever come across associated with stand-up paddleboarding. As I started training for my first (and second) race of the season, I began recording every term I've learned in the past year of SUP. I've tried to be as inclusive as I can, but also feel like every time I go out on the water I think of a new term (today it was "sunglasses", "croakies", and "helmet"). Therefore, this is a constantly evolving glossary just like the sport of stand-up paddleboarding itself. Enjoy.

Chapter 1- 101 Tips, Tricks, and Terms about Stand-Up Paddleboarding from A-Z

A Dictionary of Paddleboarding Terms from A-Z

Welcome to this all-inclusive guide with all tips, tricks, and terms related to stand-up paddleboarding. In this book you will find everything I could ever think of in regards to SUP's health benefits, equipment, advice, suggestions, and what has worked for me in mastering the art of stand-up paddleboarding.

Here you'll find a true dictionary with every letter of the alphabet covered with terms associated with stand-up paddleboarding (and more). Keep in mind though that this A to Z guide contains my personal interpretation related to SUP and may not be true to the meanings in the Webster's Dictionary. Stand-up paddleboarding is evolving so quickly that new terms are popping up constantly.

Please keep in mind that this is a basic overview of stand-up paddleboarding with tips and a glossary born from a first person perspective...meaning that this is primarily coming from a beginner paddleboarder like me who is pretty new to the sport. However, since I work in a SUP rental shop/cafe surrounded by elite paddlers and people who are equally passionate about the sport, you will also find some emotions and companies that I associate with stand-up paddleboarding, too.

And 101 Tips and Tricks to How to Become a Better Paddleboarder

Plus, in this book you will find 101 tips and tricks hidden throughout the chapters and in the terms. Since this book has "101 Secrets, Lessons and Tips" in the title, they are bolded, numbered, and highlighted in red throughout the book.

There are also chapters covering broad topics, such as an Intro into SUP and Health Benefits from SUP. All of these terms and ideas are related to each other, but the meat of the book is in the glossary. I hope you learn something new, remember something you forgot, or feel inspired with some of the terms and tips in this book.

The Top Three Things You Need to Be a Decent Stand-Up Paddleboarder

Before we get into the meat of this book, know that **(Tip #1) safety should be at the forefront of all of your paddling adventures**. This means that you need to always be prepared with the right equipment and accessories and stay within your ability level. No matter what kind of waterway you are on, you should always have a life jacket/PFD and try to paddle with other people as often as you can. Other accessories such as a leash, dry bag with necessities, and emergency signal devices can be helpful to have too. These terms are highlighted throughout the book, but here are three main things I believe will also help you enjoy the sport:

1) Balance- What I love about stand-up paddleboarding is that it forces you to work on your balance because you are on a constantly changing surface. Coming from a wakeboarding/snowboarding/skateboarding background, SUP and yoga (or a combination of both) forces me to work with nature to stay upright on the board. I also love the feeling of "walking on water" while getting a full body workout in.

2) Mindset- Being connected to nature and the water can also give you a sense of peace and overall wellbeing. I think a big part of enjoying paddleboarding is to **(Tip #2) not be afraid of falling in the water.** I actually think it's kind of fun to try new balancing moves and fall in to cool off. Remember whatever you are doing on your SUP the main goal should be to have FUN and embrace the challenges. Just make sure you are prepared with the right type of clothing and equipment for the environment in which you will be paddling in.

3) Strength- One of the main benefits of stand-up paddleboarding is developing your strength. A reason why this sport is so popular is because as you glide across the water getting a full workout in, you are developing your strength in your legs and your core (through balancing) and your arms and shoulders by paddling and gaining momentum. As you paddle more and more, you will naturally build up your strength that will help you get back on your board faster, paddle more confidently through rough conditions, and do better in SUP competitions.

11

Chapter 2- An Intro into Stand-Up Paddleboarding

The Equipment You Need

What is stand-up paddleboarding, exactly? Derived from the surfing world, SUP has been around for centuries as people from coastal areas used stand-up paddleboarding as a means for travelling between islands, fishing, and surfing. In recent times (especially in the last two decades), surfers started stand-up paddleboarding to easily catch more waves because they could have a better vantage point to see farther out into the horizon.

People who absolutely love the water will do anything to enjoy it, though, so what did surfers do when there weren't any waves? They grabbed a stand-up paddleboard to cruise around in the flats. Over the last two decades or so, stand-up paddleboarding exploded in popularity as people realized that it could be done not only in oceans but in lakes, rivers, and bays. Plus, it provides a low-impact, high-reward fitness workout by it being a proven way to get in shape, recover from an injury, and create a healthier mindset. In the early 2000's, studies showed that SUP was the number one outdoor recreational activity for first timers, but people who live close to inland lakes and other waterways (like myself) have found and implemented paddleboarding into their daily lifestyle.

<u>(Tip #3)</u> **To SUP, you need a board, a paddle, a life jacket (also known as a PFD), a leash, and an open mind.** Those are the basics, and then as you

get more into it, depending on what you're doing, or how much time you're spending on the water, then you may want take a dry bag, waterproof watch, or other accessories. That all comes with experience and how committed you are to paddleboarding. If it's something that you really want to get into, I suggest trying out different boards and figuring out what's comfortable before you jump in and buy. Paddleboards are evolving all the time and you want to be sure that you're happy with your investment and that it has quality materials and durability to last you a while.

Proper Paddle Technique

If you are brand-new to paddleboarding, there are definitely some things to keep in mind to truly enjoy the sport. Waves, boat chop, and variable weather conditions are just a few things that can affect your steadiness and balance, so it's good to start small and build up your strength and mobility.

(Tip #4) When getting onto the board, start out in the center (by the vent) on your knees with the tip or point of the board in front of you and your paddle in hand. Kneeling on the board, your hands should be on the shaft of the paddle and the blade facing forward. To get around, you dip the blade into the water and pull it towards you to get momentum.

Once you feel comfortable paddling on your knees, then stand up. Maintaining balance, place one hand on the handle of your paddle and keep the other wrapped around the middle of the shaft. You'll probably want to paddle 3-5 strokes on each side before switching arms and depending on which direction you're headed.

(Tip #5) Quickblade, a leading manufacturer of SUP paddles, released a tip sheet called the Phases of the Stroke which include the Catch, Power Phase, Exit, and Recovery. These paddle stroke terms are explained throughout the glossary. Mastering proper paddling technique will help prevent risk of injury and help you become a faster and more confident paddler.

Water Safety

Mother Nature can be brutal sometimes, and so (Tip #6) you always want to be prepared for changing water conditions, weather, or anything that may come up that's out of your control. Especially when it's just you, the open water, and your paddleboard (which is why you should always paddle with other people whenever possible). Practicing proper water safety at all times can be the key between life and death if you happen to find yourself in a dangerous situation. These are emphasized in the glossary, but I will point out again some tips to stay safe no matter what kind of waters you're in:

(Tip #7) Always wear (or at least have) a leash. A leash is designed to keep you attached to the board...exactly how it sounds, it is usually comprised of a Velcro strap that wraps around your ankle, has a coil, and attaches to the board. It gives you flexibility to move around on the board while ensuring that your board is always close by.

Wearing a leash at all times is required when paddleboarding in the United States. A Coast Guard-approved PFD can stay on your board (you do not have to be wearing it), but in case you get separated from your board and need access to your life jacket, a leash will help you get back to it to be able to put on your life jacket and be able to call for safety.

There have been some instances when people feel uncomfortable wearing a leash when paddling in rivers or places where it can get tangled up in rocks or underwater obstacles. In these types of waterways, you should wear a breakaway leash that attaches to your waist and can't hold you down preventing you from reaching the water's surface.

(Tip #8) Always have a Coast Guard-approved life jacket on or near you. In the US, it is a requirement to have a life jacket either on you or on your paddleboard at all times. The standard life jacket that you probably see everywhere is a bright orange floating device, usually tucked into the traps on the bow of your vessel.

I usually don't wear a life jacket while paddleboarding because I like to have more mobility, but when you're just starting out and unsure of what you're doing, it can make you feel more at ease to wear your life jacket until you get more comfortable in the water. There have been many times when the wind has kicked up on Lake Tahoe, the place where I mainly paddle, and I've had to put in all of my effort to get back to shore.

I've definitely felt better knowing that I had a life jacket close by and that my orange floaty was easy to see (and had a whistle on it) just in case I needed to use it.

(Tip #9) **Recently I just upgraded my life jacket to a manual waist vest for flatwater paddling to have more mobility.** I've been paddling regularly for a few months now and I noticed SUP racers had this funny little fanny pack thing around their waist that is actually a life jacket. When needed, you can pull the string attached to the waist vest and it releases CO_2 into a floatation device (much like what you see on an airplane). It really is perfect for racing because you barely notice it's there.

At least on my lake, the Coast Guard does do random checks to make sure you have a life jacket. Usually they can tell from afar when you have a big orange vest strapped to your board, but the tiny waist packs can be a bit more subtle and they may ask you about it.

(Tip #10) **In a dangerous situation, don't let your paddle hold you up.** My friend Jay Wild, owner of Waterman's Landing, and I were talking about this the other day- when people get thrown off their board unexpectedly, they tend to hold onto their paddle at the risk of drowning. I don't know why this is... I think it might be natural instinct to not want to let go for fear that your paddle will sink to the bottom.*

However, in this case your paddle is probably holding you back and your life is more important. Get rid of the paddle and concentrate on getting back to your

16

board first. Once you can remount your vessel, put on your life jacket and use your arms to paddle back to your paddle. Fortunately, many newer paddles are lightweight and made of carbon fiberglass material that floats.

(Tip #11) **Paddle with friends.** I love paddling with other people because I'm always learning new things and I just feel a lot better having a buddy watch my back.

Stand-up paddleboarding is better with friends.

* I recently just watched that Red Bull video of a motocross rider taking his dirt bike in the ocean; in one instance he missed the on-water ramp and started sinking with his very expensive toy. I can see not wanting to let go of a $20,000 dirt bike that you just put a ton of money and time into even when you're drowning, but I still feel that your life is more important (and anything you lose can always be recovered later, right?) So just remember, if you need your arms to swim and stay afloat, a paddle is way less expensive to replace than a dirt bike in the ocean.

Although reading about these safety tips is a good start, it's always best to practice these in action. Many SUP shops offer lessons and demos; I highly advise getting a refresher course at the start of every season unless you are practicing safety guidelines on the water regularly already.

How to Turn

Once you're standing up on the paddleboard and cruising along confidently, at some point you may want to turn...to get back to shore, to veer away from a motorboat, or to get around a buoy, or to line yourself up to paddle straight through the waves. Here are four basic ways to turn that friends and experts have told me about:

(Tip #12) With a C-Stroke: Keeping one hand on the handle and one hand on the shaft of the paddle, reach as far as you can forward and do a wide sweeping stroke, creating as much space as you can between you and the board. This will help turn the board slow and steady.

(Tip #13) Coming to an Abrupt Halt: Say you want to turn left, and you want to do it now, then the quickest way to make that happen is to poke the blade into the water and push against the water, adding a bit of resistance and causing the board to whip around in the direction in which you have the blade. Although this isn't the most efficient way to turn in a race because you lose all momentum, it works to turn.

When you are first starting out, these are by far the easiest ways to turn and then you can progress up. When I first started paddleboarding, it took me at least a few months to master the C/sweeping stroke (and I'm still not sure if I have it right). However, in my first two SUP races, it was always the buoy turns that held me up...I would be head-to-head with another competitor and then they would gain the lead at the buoy. In a race, I lost time when my C-stroke was too wide and the paddle poke technique caused me to lose all momentum. With a few months of training under my belt, I soon graduated to practicing these types of turns:

(Tip #14) The Crossbow: This has been my favorite one to practice, because I feel like there's still a lot to learn. My understanding of it is that you want to bring your whole paddle to the opposite side of the board and pull your body towards it, creating resistance towards the nose of your board. What I like about this stroke is that it whips you around while still moving forward and not losing the momentum you would from an abrupt halt.

(Tip #15) Moving Your Body Back (combined with the C-stroke): Another way to turn is to change your body positioning on the board and making your paddle like a rudder. If you move your feet back, then you're creating more surface area in front of you. The nose of your board will start to rise as you put more weight towards the back of it and with the tip out of the water you will naturally turn faster in the direction of which you paddle. However, it takes a lot of balance to move your feet around on the board without toppling over- this is an advanced move that takes some practice. I've tried to practice this by placing my paddle in the center of the board for stability and shuffling my feet back until I get to a point on it where it could make a difference in my turns. It's slight, but something I'm working on. **(Tip #16) Practicing yoga on a SUP also helps with balance and not being afraid to fall in the water.**

How to Remount (Getting Back on Your Board When You Fall Into the Water)

I'm going to tell you now that (Lesson #17) falling in the water is inevitable with paddleboarding, especially if you're trying to teach your dog how to balance on the board with you. So when it happens, how in the world do you get back on? If you find yourself all of the sudden wet and next to the board instead of on top of it, don't panic. Simply swim to the center of the board (flip it over if you need to so that the grip padding is on top and the fin is in the water), grab onto it, and pull yourself up onto your belly, then eventually swing your butt around or get on your knees. The other way is to go the tail of the board and grab either side of it and pull yourself up onto it (like how you would mount a surfboard or a boogie board). Personally, I put my paddle up on the board first and then crawl back on top of it by the center when I'm nice and cooled off (or climb back up on it as fast as I can if I don't want anyone to know I fell in).

Sit down on your board and take a break if you need to.

Chapter 3- Health Benefits From Stand-Up Paddleboarding

Why Stand-Up Paddleboarding Is Good For Your Mind, Body, and Soul

There are a whole bunch of reasons why stand-up paddleboarding is a popular sport. Being on or near water invokes a sense of peacefulness and calm mainly because you are connected with nature and soaking in the benefits of being outside. Plus, stand-up paddleboarding provides a low impact, full-body workout that's great for creating better posture and lessening pain from previous injuries mainly in the lower back and core.

Why Proper Technique Is Important

While there are many great benefits to stand-up paddleboarding, you can take on some bad habits in technique that can lead to injury or joint pain rather than fix it (one of the most common injuries in paddleboarding are strained shoulders). **(Tip #18) Invest in the right equipment and take a class to learn how to properly paddle right from the get-go**, and pick up tips from fellow paddlers on how to safely deal with a challenging environment.

Working with a trusted coach or trainer will also teach you how to gain the maximum fitness benefits while out on the water.

www.supadventurer.com

The first step to get anywhere on a SUP? Learn how to hold the paddle.

Ever Experience Numb Feet? Here's Why and How to Fix 'Em

I remember when I first started paddleboarding (and after I took a break from it for a couple of months and got back into it again), I experienced numb feet while paddleboarding and would have to stop and take a break. But then it slowly went away as I spent more time out on the water. I wanted to address this here because I know that other people experience it, too. So before you give up on the sport due to your feet feeling like they are going to fall off, take a look at why that might be happening:

It is pretty common for many beginner stand-up paddleboarders to experience cramping or hurting in their feet because as you work to stay balanced on the board you may inadvertently be gripping your toes, working out muscles you never knew you had. **(Tip #19) So to keep your feet from cramping up, remember to relax your toes and wiggle them around a little bit, or try to shift your weight front and back to keep the blood flowing in your feet.**

A more advanced move to prevent numb feet is to move your body around on the board. However, moving one foot at a time and favoring one side of the board will cause you to be unbalanced. In the YouTube SUP Tips video by Blue Planet Surf, Robert suggests making little jumps forward and back to stretch out your feet. Bending your knees and changing the positioning of your feet (as long as you're not rocking the board) can also help relax stiff joints.

Personally, I try to put the paddle in the middle of the board to offer some stability when trying to shift my weight around (but I admit that's probably not good for digging the paddle into the board).

What to Eat Before, During and After Paddleboarding

Much like how we plug our iPhones in to recharge them when the battery is getting low, we use food to sustain our energy and give us power to get through our paddle sessions. Therefore, what we put in our bodies is pretty important. A balanced diet filled with grains, fruits, vegetables, nuts, dairy, and poultry are all good basics to implement into your meal plan to complement your various outdoor activities. It also helps to pay attention to organic and locally-sourced food (the farm-to-table approach) and try to ingest naturally-produced, organic fare that is as pure as possible.

At Waterman's Landing, the café/paddleboard rental shop I work at in Lake Tahoe, the café side of it serves local organic coffee, turkey and ham free of nitrates or nitrites, and housemade blueberry scones, bacon jam, and salad dressings. While its menu has all sorts of breakfast and lunch items that appeal to a larger demographic of people besides paddleboarders, I started to notice that our regular watermen and women seemed to veer towards items that are consistent with the paleo diet. Before going out on the water, I even found myself wanting to pop a Paleo Ball- a rolled up mixture of coconut oil, butter, cacao, and coffee. After getting off of the water, I wanted an acai bowl (acai berry chocked with antioxidants on a bed of granola) or a gluten-free granola bar (which one customer calls "paleo bricks"). Bullet coffees are also gaining more popular (coffee with butter and coconut oil in it).

I started to wonder why paddlers are so drawn to the paleo diet and talked to fellow health fanatics about it. It's pretty simple why people who are into fitness and exercise like it- because it gets back to the root of food. The paleo diet focuses on original foods that our ancestors ate, free of harmful toxins and preservatives and is full of heart-healthy fats that combat cardiovascular and autoimmune diseases, while giving one the energy they need to stay strong and maintain stamina.

As you get more into paddleboarding, you will probably notice how foods affect your energy levels and body. I look at it like training for a trail race- you probably don't want to load up on heavy sugary foods the night before because you don't want risk getting cramps or experiencing a crash, affecting your performance in the 10k or halfway through the marathon. I think this applies to paddleboarding, too, except that it's a bit harder to get food or replenish what you need when you're doing long distances out on the water. That's why I think it's important to pay attention to what you are putting into your body before your next paddling session.

Nutrition Coach Scott Estrada said that while paddleboarding, **(Tip #20) you want to take foods paddling that are easy to carry and remember to stay hydrated.** Personally, one of his top paddling snacks includes dates.

"They are an amazing energy source, they have 60-plus minerals in them and store glucose. Plus, they stash well on a board and are still edible when wet (and they don't sink). They pack a punch and travel well on the water," he says. **(Tip #21) Estrada will**

even replace the pits of his dates with macadamia nuts or walnuts.

"It's like any other sport, the fuel you need to put into your body. Think of foods that are easy to digest- you don't want the blood caught in your stomach when it needs to be in your head," Estrada says.

Some experts say that complex carbohydrates such as beans, oats, and other grains can gradually help the body release energy rather than a quick surge caused by a donut (which is more likely to leave you depleted sooner than you may have intended).

Heart-healthy foods and essential fatty acids found in fish and certain plants can also help lubricate joints in the body, regulate oxygen use, increase mental sharpness (have you ever heard the advice to eat fish when studying for a test?), and assist blood cells in fighting infections. Many of these food attributes are available in the paleo diet and directly affect performance which is why many elite athletes and people seeking a healthier lifestyle are concerned about what they put in their bodies.

"The cleaner you eat the better you're going to perform," Estrada says. "It's getting back to the primal foods and thank goodness that's finally catching on. The marketing on processed foods is powerful and you really have to pay attention to what you're putting in your body, look at real nourishment. We're at the worst diseases in our culture and it has to go back to our food- the intake and exposure," he adds.

Food that has protein, is packed with nutrients, and containing essential fatty acids that help you keep your strength up during your paddle sessions are the best to keep around, but it's also important to drink water or stay hydrated. When you're out there in the sun all day exercising, it's easy to work up a sweat.

While I'm totally advocating for the paleo diet, I do think that you should find what works for you and recognize how food affects your body; especially doing a high-intensity sport or sign up for a long distance paddling session.

Chapter 4- Terms From A-I Related to Stand-Up Paddleboarding

Words Like Accelerating, Balance, Conditioning

Ability, Acceleration, A-frame, Altitude, Accountability, Awareness, Attitude, Agility, Acai Bowl

Ability: **(Tip #21) How good you are at paddleboarding all depends on how much time you spend out on the water.** Participating in other watersports and being comfortable in lakes, rivers, and the ocean definitely helps. Plus, if you are already moderately active or a reasonably fit person than you already have a head start in your ability to paddle. Sometimes SUP events list what level you need to be at in order to participate and keep everyone safe, which would be a good to take a moment to examine your own strengths and weaknesses. For instance, maybe you wake up and decide that you want to do a 22-mile inland lake race...how prepared are you for that? Have you entered other races of varying distances and if so, how did it go? Taking lessons or getting a good coach is the best way to improve your ability level and paddling skills especially if you are looking at entering an intense race.

Acai Bowl: I believe that your diet is a big part of being comfortable and confident out on the water. At

Waterman's Landing, the paddleboard rental shop/café that I work at, we introduced a new acai bowl on the menu that is perfect to consume before or after a paddle. Comprised of four ounces of pure acai berry mixed with banana atop of homemade granola, it has all of the antioxidants and energy you need to get you through the next few hours out on the water; it's also the perfect filling snack for when you get back. One guy came in after paddling 20 miles from South Lake Tahoe to North Shore (it took him seven hours) and he said that the acai bowl and a smoothie got him up and functioning again.

Acceleration: Accelerating on a SUP can be attributed to a few different things, but mainly it all has to do with your ability level, technique, and equipment. I started out on a board that was great for touring and offered a lot of stability, but tended to drag in the water. When I began training this season, I started taking out lighter, skinnier boards that would just glide without putting in any effort. As you improve and gain more strength out on the water, then I would say that your equipment plays a big role in your ability to accelerate and beat other people out in the water.

Accountability: **(Tip #22) If you're training for a paddleboard race, having a coach, a team, or at least a paddling buddy is a great way to get better because they can provide some accountability,** a.k.a. making sure you are staying on track to reach your goals. The reason why I got into racing is because I enjoy being in a competitive atmosphere with people who love paddleboarding as much as I do. Sometimes I have to be accountable to myself when I set goals and have to follow through, but even sharing my goals or plans with other people can help me stay focused.

Agility: Men's Journal published an article a while back about in-the-gym exercises you can do to help improve your agility on a paddleboard. **(Tip #23) Kneeling pulldown to triceps arm presses and rowing machines can help you improve your arm strength while using a balance ball or exercise board can help with your overall balance.** There are many cross-training exercises for paddleboarding that you can practice as well to help improve your agility- going on a long run can help with your endurance and reducing fatigue while yoga can help your balance. Improving the ability to move, think, and understand quickly and easily is not only a goal in paddleboarding but can apply to many other aspects of life in any situation where you need to be quick on your feet.

A-Frame: **(Tip #24) When paddling, I've been told that you want to keep one arm out in front of you with your hand on top of the handle and your other arm placed halfway down in a comfortable position on the shaft, keeping your arms in an "A-Frame" position on the board.** Keep your arms fairly straight in front of you (except when you're bending your elbow in the recovery) and try to maintain a consistent form.

Altitude: Where you are training makes a big difference in how much energy you have in a race or just touring around. I paddle in an alpine lake at 6200 feet above sea level, therefore I feel like I crush it in races at sea level where I have more oxygen. That's why training in a place like Lake Tahoe is great for not only paddling, but for running, mountain bike riding, swimming and other human-powered sports.

Attitude: **(Tip #25) A lot of understanding and getting better at paddleboarding all comes down to your attitude and mindset**, which I refer to a lot in this book. Not everyone is going to be a pro their first time on the water- you have to be open-minded, willing to take risks, listen to your fellow paddlers if you want to get better), and be respectful Mother Nature. Humility and humbleness are good character strengths to have also while trying to improve at paddleboarding- when you hit some boat waves and get flung off your board it always seems to be a surprise, but those types of events are learning experiences. Practicing SUP yoga also helps you challenge yourself as you develop balance and try out more advanced poses while not being afraid to fall in the water.

Awareness: **(Tip #26) I look at this as a safety tip- always be aware of your surroundings.** On the big open lake that I paddle on, the wind can kick up fast and strong. I am constantly checking Windfinder.com to see what kind of weather to expect when I'm on the water- how windy it's supposed to be at certain times of the day, what the air/water temperature is supposed to be, and what direction the wind is blowing. On rivers, you probably want to read the water depth levels and how strong the current is in certain sections. In the ocean, be aware of how strong you are as a swimmer, how big the waves are, how you are going to paddle over them, and your confidence level in getting back to shore.

I live on a big, blue alpine lake where objects are farther away than they appear. When I first started paddling, I thought that going from Waterman's Landing to Dollar Point was going to be a breeze, but was quite a distance away from my ability level at the time. A lot of people who rent paddleboards at the shop want to jump in and head towards the middle of the lake, but a good rule of thumb is to only go the distance that you're comfortable swimming back. That is so in the worst case scenario if you lose your board, your paddle, and no one is around to rescue you, the only thing you can do is swim back to shore.

People also don't realize how cold the water can be in the off-months (in Lake Tahoe) and when they fall off their paddleboard then hypothermia can set in fast. Therefore, when I want to go out on the calm, glassy lake in the middle of April when the water temperature is 44 degrees, I'm sure to tell at least one other person where I'm paddling and how long I expect to be gone. (Remember the movie *127 Hours* about climber Aron Ralston who took off into the Utah desert and got stuck in a crevice for days? I bet he wished he had told someone where he was going.)

Prepare for your outdoor adventure whether it's for an hour, a day, or a week and pay attention to the weather and your surroundings once you're there.

B- Buoy Turns, Basics, Balance, Barnacle speaker, Blown out, Boat Chop, Back stroke, Breakaway Leash

Back stroke: Many people are so concentrated on going forward that they forget about their back stroke (which I liken to riding switch on a snowboard or wakeboard). It's a bit uncomfortable because it's not practiced as often, but when you do it helps improve your overall paddling skills. **(Tip #27) To do a back stroke, you first want to see what's behind you (believe it or not, many times people don't watch where they're going and they back into something). Then you want to put the blade of the paddle into the water behind your hip and pull it towards your body.** Remember to look over your shoulder every once in a while to see where you're headed. The back stroke is fun to practice because it works out different muscle groups and can help prevent shoulder injuries or dislocation from forward stroking all the time. However, there are also other on-land exercises that you can do to relieve strain on your shoulders (like the cactus exercise by putting your arms up in the air in a 90-degree angle on either side).

Balance: Paddleboarding is great for developing balance because it requires that you maintain a standing position on an uneven surface (the water) which is in turn working every muscle in your body. I find that even when I'm a bit stressed or just feel a bit emotionally thrown off, simply being out in the water and working on my balance on a paddleboard can help reset my mind. Like yoga, SUP is a low-impact sport that can help you lose weight and become healthier, which all comes back to working on your balance.

Barnacle speaker: I just threw this in here because it's a paddleboard accessory that I really want to get soon. I love listening to music on the water and a Barnacle is a waterproof wireless outdoor speaker about the size of a fist that can be stuck on your paddleboard, raft, or dashboard of your boat. With a Barnacle, you can Bluetooth to dial in your favorite music, throw your smartphone in your dry bag, and glide away. It is dust proof, it floats, and it lasts up to five hours. I am getting one this year.

Basics: Getting back to paddleboarding, I find that it's helpful to understand the basics of paddleboarding by taking a lesson or going out with a friend or two who can give you some tips. The first time I went paddleboarding was with a few girls, and we just played around and had fun on the water, and none of us cared what our form looked like or how often we fell in. I feel like I picked it up pretty fast because I had 20 years' worth of experience waterskiing, wakeboarding, and surfing, but for those that need a little extra guidance then keep in mind that many paddleboard shops that are close to the water offer lessons and clinics for how to improve. I find that going out on the water with other people always helps.

Blown out: I can't remember where I first heard this term, but I know that when a body of water is super choppy due to wind and you see whitecap waves, then it's referred to as being "blown out".

Boat Chop: This term refers to waves that are caused from a boat's wake, which can affect your balance and stability on the board. (Tip #28) **When boats drive by and gigantic waves are rippling your way, I find that it's best to directly face them head-on, paddling through them or up and over them.** If you don't paddle through them, then the waves may spin you around so that you're parallel to them and then will dump you into the water. (Tip #29) **When you see the waves coming towards you and are afraid you can't get through them, get in a kneeling position and paddle through them.** It also helps to stick close to the shoreline to alleviate any big wakes (US states have certain laws about how far motorboats have to stay from the shore) and try to be as visible as possible to any oncoming boats by waving your paddle in the air or orange flotation device if you have one.

Breakaway Leash: When I entered my first river race, I wondered whether I would need a leash. I've heard that a few accidents have occurred from people who fell off of their board and their leash got snagged on rocks or debris and kept them under. A breakaway leash allows you to easily disconnect from your board, which ideal for paddling in a river where you're dealing with currents.

Buoy Turns: Usually SUP races have at least one or two turns in them and getting around them keeping your momentum and trying to beat out your competitor can be a bit tricky. It's twice now that I've been head-to-head with someone in a SUP race and they beat me out in the buoy turn and then kept the lead. There are a few different ways to master a buoy turn such as backing up on the board, practicing the wide/C-stroke, the crossbow turn, or poking your paddle in the water to stop the board and whip it around.

C- Comradery, Coaching, Cruising, Clothing, Catch, Clinic, Conditioning, Calluses, Carbon fiber, Calm Water, Crunches, Cardio, Crossbow Turn, Currents, C-Stroke, Croakies

C-stroke: **(Tip #30) Also called a wide stroke, this paddling method is a good one to practice for buoy turns and generally making a fast turn in the direction you want to go.** To do it, reach your paddle out and in the catch, sweep it out as far away as you can from your body. The board should start to turn in direction where you want to be headed. To turn around a buoy, I've noticed that a combination of the C-stroke/wide stroke and the crossbow stroke is the best way to make a turn and keep your momentum.

Calluses: Unfortunately with SUPing, calluses are pretty common to get within your palms depending on how often and how hard you paddle. However, like with any sport, you get used to them. If you don't want to deal with calluses or simply want to be more comfortable, then companies like Yakgrips create paddle grips that are insulated and can help people keep their hands in the right position while lessening the pressure on your hands.

Calm water: This is the best type of water to go paddling in. I'm fortunate to live close to an inland lake that has glassy water mornings and evenings, but a lot of the times it is super early in the morning or late at night (calm water in the wakeboarding world is also called "butter"). **(Tip #31) I check the Windfinder app to see when the best water is.** Calm water can also be found in bays, marinas, and stagnant parts of rivers.

Cardio: What's great about stand-up paddleboarding is that it provides a low-impact workout that can also be as physically demanding as other board sports such as surfing or wakeboarding. Whether you are using your paddleboard to do yoga, go down a river, go fishing, or scoot your dog around on the lake, you are getting a cardio workout in. **(Tip #32) For people who want to burn fat, cardio workouts that are more than 15 minutes long will give you the most benefit-** moderate aerobic exercise burns off calories that can help shed pounds and reach fitness goals. To support your workout, consider paddling with a heart monitor (my waterproof Garmin Vivo comes with a chest monitor) to track your intensity and adjust your training schedule to get the maximum cardiovascular benefits.

Carbon fiber: The original best, sturdiest paddleboards have traditionally been made with fiberglass but as they've evolved, SUP makers have been trying to find ways to create boards that are lighter, faster, and are durable in any kind of water conditions. When I started racing, I used a fiberglass board that was kind of heavy and cumbersome to handle and eventually reached a point where I felt drag due to the construction of the board. Then I got on a full carbon fiber board and noticed that it was lighter and easily glided through the water without having to put in much effort. With a carbon fiber SUP, I've shaved 1-2 minutes off of my paddle time.

Catch: The "catch" refers to the first phase of the 4-phase paddle stroke demonstrated by Quickblade, which is the start of the stroke the send the blade first hits the water. **(Tip #33) Quickblade suggests that in the catch you want to submerge the blade of the paddle completely in the water before pulling it towards you.** To move forward, extend your arm out as comfortable as it will go but don't try to overdo it. (Your positioning should look like the A-frame.)

Clinic- **(Tip #34) Taking a SUP clinic held by trusted expert is one of the best ways to get better at stand-up paddleboarding.** Some SUP shops just offer rentals, but some host clinics and lessons as well- it's best just to Google shops in your area and see what's out there. Visiting SUP shops and going to races will also allow you to meet people and get recommendations on the best instruction. Taking a clinic/lesson/refresher with a good coach can help you get rid of any bad habits and paddle with maximum efficiency. However, if you are training for an event or a race then keep in mind that taking just one or two clinics or lessons is not going to make you become a pro- you have put in as much time as you can on the water and practice to get better over time.

Clothing- What is the right thing to wear paddleboarding? Many people who paddleboard in the ocean may wear a wetsuit if the water's cold, but if you are in a stagnant, calm body of water like an inland lake or even a river, then **(Tip #35) you probably want to wear something light and**

breathable. I usually wear what I would if I were to do some kind of sport on land- yoga pants, a sports bra/bikini top, tank top, and a light long-sleeved shirt if it's cold outside. I want clothing that will dry quickly if I fall in the water and will be tolerable if I work up a sweat. Usually I see guys out there in board shorts and maybe a rash guard or dry fit tank tops.

Coaching- **(Tip #36) If you are training for a race or have a particular goal related to stand-up paddleboarding, then a coach or a trainer can help you** come up with a tailored training plan, diet, and accountability. I remember when I first started paddleboarding and I wanted to enter a race, I had no idea where to start. Fortunately, I work at a paddleboard rental shop/café with two elite paddleboarders who could guide me in setting realistic goals, advice on what to eat, and let me demo equipment that was appropriate for my race. For a 3-mile race, they recommended that I do at least 4-5 days a week of on-water workouts for four weeks and it worked- that helped me build the muscles I needed to meet my goal in the race. Especially for a long-distance paddle (like a marathon), a coach or trainer can help keep you motivated, offer continual guidance, and be there to help you celebrate the successes.

Comradery- My favorite thing about paddleboarding is the comradery between fellow paddlers. I've met the nicest, happiest, fittest people through paddleboarding whether it's from a race, a clinic, travelling or through Waterman's Landing- the paddleboard rental shop/café I work at. I've met so many people who share the same love of the water and also learned a lot about fitness, diet, and overall wellbeing primarily through SUP. (Tip #37) You are more likely to enjoy the sport and get better at paddleboarding when you do it with other people.

Croakies: This term refers to the little band of neoprene that fits around the sides of your sunglass frames to keep you from losing your shades when they fall in the water. They are a great investment if you have a favorite pair of expensive, irreplaceable sunglasses that you don't want to risk slipping to the bottom of the lake, ocean, or river while paddling.

Cross-Training Conditioning: Weather, responsibilities, your job, and other factors can keep you from getting on the water as often as you'd like, but fortunately there are a lot of cross-training exercises that you can do off the water to help reduce fatigue, increase your endurance, and be stronger for when you do get the chance to paddle. (Tip #38) Some great conditioning exercises involve swimming because it works your core, your back and your legs as you create resistance in the water that directly translates to more efficient paddling. (Tip #39) I find that long bike rides or running long distances can also help you build stamina. I know that a few SUP coaches are also into CrossFit because it focuses on high-intensity interval training, its gyms have excellent equipment, and you get a dedicated trainer/group to keep you on track.

Crossbow Turn: I recently learned how to do this to get around buoys faster and it's an invaluable move for a race. Before, I would practice the C-stroke and create resistance in the water to whip my board around, but then that would make my board stop and my competitor would gain the lead. Fortunately at my first race of the season, I learned how my friend Nikki got ahead of me- she practiced a combination of the crossbow and the C-stroke. **(Tip #40) To do the crossbow turn, you turn your body (hips, shoulders, head) to the opposite side of the board and to bring the blade towards the nose of the board in the catch.** This move combined with the C-stroke keeps you moving forward and complete your turn more successfully. (For a full description of the crossbow turn, visit neverboredinc.com.)

Crunches: It's already been stated that stand-up paddleboarding provides a full body workout, including your core...have you ever felt that you are doing crunches standing up as you are paddling? While doing crunches laying down can cause strain on your neck and shoulders if you don't do them properly, the constant movement of contracting your core while using the paddle to move through the water on a SUP has a similar, subliminal effect. **(Tip #41) You can even take it one step further and do crunches or the yoga "boat" pose on the board if you are just hanging out on the water to work those abs a little bit harder.**

Currents: Paddleboarding in river currents adds a whole new level of excitement to the sport. I recently just paddled in a 6-mile SUP race down the Sacramento River in Northern California and I had no idea what to expect. I had done a couple of 3-mile SUP races (one in a bay and one in an inland lake) and the fastest I could paddle was averaging a 17-18 minute pace per mile. But when I entered the 6-mile river race, I did it in 57 minutes averaging a 10-minute pace (about what I average when I *run* a 5k). While not having to expend as much effort to go downwind in a river race is fun, I did have to watch out for ripples, shallow water, eddies, snags, and other river hazards. I highly recommend trying a SUP out on a river at least once in your life.

Words Like Downwind, Endurance, Feathering

D- Downwind, Deck, Displacement Hull, Diet, Dry Bag, Dock Start, Demo Boards, Dog SUP, Ducks

Deck: The term "deck" refers to the top of the paddleboard that you place your feet on. A lot of newer boards have some kind of a foam grip on the top that is comfortable for your feet, knees, and rest of your body. However, much like surfboards, there are some boards that don't have any kind of foam top. Some people use Sticky Bumps which is a wax that you spread on the board to cause some kind of soft cushion/grip for your feet. **(Tip #42) You will want to position your feet near the middle of the board or the vent/handle to have your weight equally distributed when perched on the deck of your paddleboard.**

Demo Boards: A lot of paddleboard rental shops probably lease out some standard displacement hull-type boards (for touring, racing), maybe some yoga boards (that feature a wide surface area and foamy grip), and planing hull boards (that have rounder noses like surf boards that bounce over the waves). For an adjusted price, many rental shop companies let you try out higher-end performance boards (also called demo boards) so that you can feel the difference between a standard board and one that is made with better quality materials or something specially designed for what you are trying to do. When I first started paddleboarding, I wanted to go out and get the cheapest board just to have one that I could use anytime. However, my friends at Waterman's Landing advised against it, afraid I would outgrow one of the rental boards. The day before my first race of the season, that's exactly what happened. I felt like a standard board had too much drag and no matter how much effort I put in, the board just wasn't moving forward as fast as I wanted to. For the next day's race, I demoed a 404 carbon race board and shaved about four minutes off of my pace per mile time. Now I can't go back to a standard rental board. **(Tip #43) If you seriously get into stand-up paddleboarding and are in the market to buying a high-end board, then demo a couple of different models first.**

Diet: What you put in your body to sustain your energy and stay fit has a lot to do with how you'll feel on a stand-up paddleboard. I think it's amazing how what you eat directly impacts how you'll perform. Before working at Waterman's Landing, I used to not eat well. I liked sausage, wine, pancakes, pasta, and chocolate. But then working at the café where we served all organic food- eggs, cheese, milk, coffee, no-nitrite/nitrate turkey or ham, I started noticing a major difference in my energy levels when I went out paddling and can correlate that to what I ate. For instance, if I had a donut and a soda before I went out on the water, I would have an eminent sugar crash compared to a flavored sparkling water and gluten-free granola bar that would keep me paddling strong throughout my session. **(Tip #44) So if your overall goal is to get fitter and healthier through paddleboarding, then you should care about what you eat.**

Displacement Hull: SUP boards come in several different shapes that are tailored to what you are trying to do out on the water, but the two main shapes of paddleboard hulls on the market are the planing hull board which is flat and a displacement hull board which is designed to cut through the water by displacing it on either side. It has a pointed nose, best suited for touring or racing and some depth to it, causing the water to part on either side when it meets the board. This is also a common hull shape for motorboats and ships because a displacement hull keeps the vessel gliding forward with less work. I noticed the difference between a displacement hull board and a planing hull board right off the bat when I got in choppy water- while a planing hull board bounced over the waves, a displacement hull board cut right through them.

Dock Start: There are a lot of different types of starts in a SUP race from holding your board on the beach and jumping on it at the sound of the alarm to being on the water on your board at a starting line ready to take off when you get the go-ahead. But the most advanced move I've ever seen on a paddleboard is a dock start where a paddleboard was off on the side of the dock and a rider with his paddle in hand ran down the dock and jumped on it, then effortlessly started paddling (watch the 18-second YouTube video here).

The more common way to dock start is to put your leash on first, place the board in the water, grab your paddle, sit on the edge of the dock and put your feet on the board, stay low and then kneel onto the middle of the board (placing your paddle on the board if you need to). Push away from the dock and maybe paddle a couple of times before standing up on the board (just make sure you're far enough away from the dock so that it's not in the way if you lose your balance and fall off your board). Check out this video by Rob Casey to see how to do it and also learn how to safely approach a dock. **(Tip #45) If you are interested in SUP racing, then it's a good idea to practice different starts.**

Dog SUP: If you are yearning to get out on the water and spend time with your four-legged best friend, then stand-up paddleboarding is a great way to combine your passion for SUP and your pup. Many people here in Lake Tahoe like to hike, mountain bike ride, and snow ski with their beloved pooches, so why not take them on the SUP, too? My friend Cory takes his 2-year-old golden retriever out on his SUP and she loves it. After teaching her how to sit and lay down, he placed her onto the board, coaxed her with treats and used a leash to keep her attached to the board. He was extra careful as he approached the shoreline as many dogs try to jump off. Sure, Marley sent Cory sailing into the water a few times but after lots of practice the pair got it down. It's a way for you both to practice your balance and enjoy time outside together. Some paddle shops even offer dog SUP and kayaking classes, accessories such as doggie life vests, and tips on how to SUP with your pup.

Downwind: There are many kinds of activities you can do on a paddleboard such as touring, fishing, yoga, and racing, but one of the lesser-known forms of paddleboarding is downwinding, which is when you are paddling on open water with the wind at your back. Much like surfing, it is possible to ride the waves in a downwind and have them work to your advantage. However, safety is key when going out for a downwind session. Make sure you go with experienced SUP'ers who know how to read the currents and tides, bring enough food and water for a long distance paddle, and always have a life jacket and leash. **(Tip #46) Research the water temperatures and weather conditions before you go out and have a backup plan for in case things figuratively go south (bring accessories like a cell phone/VHF radio, whistle, and light).**

Ducks: The other thing that makes me super happy when I'm out paddleboarding is all of the natural wildlife I encounter, especially ducks and geese. I see Canadian geese on many of Northern California's waterways, but have also seen jumping fish, egrets, deer, and seagulls. One of the animals I see most often, though, are the many different types of waterfowl, most of all mallards. I've seen a flock of about 20 crossing the street and hanging out in the water and on Lake Tahoe's shoreline. One morning when I went out paddleboarding, a couple came bee lining towards me, climbed up on shore, and looked at me. When they saw I didn't have anything, they preened their feathers and scooted off. I love it when I get caught up in a flock and we all paddle together. Respecting nature and seeing it in action is one of the great things about paddleboarding.

My new paddling buddies.

E- Education, Endurance, Equipment, Energy, Elastic Sports Tape, Exit, Eddy

Eddy: An eddy is defined by Dictionary.com as a small whirlpool, a current in a liquid stream that most of the time forms a whirling motion. The reason why I include it is because it is possible to get caught up in an eddy on a SUP. The first paddle I did in the Sacramento River, I went about 20 miles total and there were times when I was floating and then just wasn't moving because I got caught up in an eddy. I would have to make a cognizant effort to paddle out of it. It's a strange feeling going downstream and then all of the sudden stuck in place, but it does happen.

Education: What I love about paddleboarding is that it is constant education. Every session I take out on the water I'm learning something new- how to read water conditions, weather, improve my technique or stroke. This sport offers continuous improvement whether it's in mindset, balance, strength, or wellbeing. There's always something to get better at in stand-up paddleboarding.

Elastic Sports Tape: Elastic sports tape is a popular accessory for hardcore athletes who need some extra muscle/tendon/ligament support while doing the sport(s) they love. When a part of the body aches or is injured, then lymphatic fluids may build up in the tissues causing swelling or inflammation. The increased pressure on your joints is felt through significant soreness or pain. When applied correctly, elastic sports tape can decompress fascia layers and allow the lymphatic fluid to move freely while also disposing of inner bacteria and cellular debris.

Endurance: Improving your endurance is a big part of paddleboarding, especially when it comes to racing, being competitive, and working towards your overall fitness. (**Tip #47**) **If you are training for a SUP race then you should y work on your muscular endurance through strength exercises.** There is a lot you can do to increase your endurance on and off the water, which can help you become less fatigued in a long distance race. For instance, mixing up your on-water training with a long distance bike ride can help you work different muscle groups while building strength. A coach or trainer can also help guide you in the right direction when it comes to endurance training and reaching your goals.

Energy: In physics, energy is present when physical work is being performed and can be converted into different forms including chemical energy, kinetic energy, and heat. Dealing with water resistance and trying to move the paddleboard definitely requires work, and your energy is changing while paddleboarding. I find that if I go paddleboarding on a regular basis, then my overall energy goes up. I sleep better, feel more relaxed, and have a better overall sense of wellbeing.

Equipment: Equipment generally refers to the paddleboard and the paddle- the absolute necessities needed to do the sport- but it can also be applied to any specialty accessories you need for what you're trying to do. For instance, if you entering a SUP race and you need your "equipment", it can include the board, the paddle, the leash, the fin, and maybe even a dry bag depending on how far you're going. If you plan on fishing off of your SUP, then equipment can also include a tackle box and a fishing rod.

Exit: Considered the third phase of the paddle stroke according to Quickblade, the "exit" is the end of the stroke when your paddle comes out of the water after the Power phase. **(Tip #48) Just make sure that the paddle exits at your feet and don't go beyond**- that will save energy because the board won't decelerate as much between strokes and you can begin your next stroke sooner.

F- Four o' Four, Feathering, Fin, Fishing, Fatigue, Full Body Workout, Focus, Fun, Facebook, Freebird Thailand

Facebook: I mention Facebook in a SUP book because this is a great resource to find out about group paddles and events in your area. **(Tip #49) Along with Facebook, I check Paddleguru.com and Google to see what's going on in the paddle community.** It was through Facebook that I found out about the Sundial Splash, a 6-mile paddle race and fun float in the Sacramento River, and now I'm always seeing group paddle outings pop up in my feed. Paddling with other people will help you become a better paddler and connected to likeminded individuals also passionate about the sport of SUP.

Fatigue: Fatigue happens when one is expending a lot of energy paddleboarding, either training for a race or going longer distances out of one's comfort zone. Fortunately, there are some things a paddler can do to reduce fatigue and mainly it comes down to practice, practice, practice. When I first started training for a 3-mile race, I was winded after a mile. But with time, I got stronger and a couple of months later paddling a mile became a breeze. For days that you can't get out on the water, running or biking long distances can also help you increase your endurance.

Feathering: When I entered my first race in the fall of 2017 in the San Francisco Bay Area, Mike Wang of Mike's Paddle shop taught me about feathering. Feathering a SUP paddle makes your stroke more efficient and less taxing on your body. **(Tip #50) In** the fourth "recovery" phase of your stroke, you want to flick your wrist on the shaft inward so that the blade is more vertical-facing, appearing "feathered" and creating less wind resistance on the return. When you feather the blade on the return, you can relax your shoulders and body for a second between strokes. Want to see a video about how feathering is done? Check out this video on it by paddling.com.

Fin: Just like in surfing, a fin (or three) on the underpart of the tail end your board keeps you stable and maintaining a specific direction. Fins come in all shapes, sizes, and can be made of different materials such as bamboo, plastic, carbon fiberglass, and epoxy. Companies create fins that are made out of recycled materials thus better for the environment and fins that swear will help you keep speed during direction changes and buoy turns. SUP fins can be anywhere from 3 to 9.75" long and are usually light, durable and aid in glide and flexibility.

Fishing: When I first paddled down the Sacramento River, I was watching fish jump a foot away from my board and thought it was amazing. In the early mornings and evenings on Lake Tahoe, I sometimes see bubbles rising to the surface while the water just reeks of fish. It is totally possible to fish on a SUP and you probably will have better luck than the fishermen in a motorized boat because you are quieter and have a better vantage point standing up. Bungee straps/netting attached to the front of your board can help keep in your tackle box, fishing license, and your fishing rod. If you're really into fishing and stand-up paddleboarding, check out these fishing paddles.

Focus: Stand-up paddleboarding requires a lot focus because there are many external factors that can affect your balance and safety on the board. For instance, you may start off a paddle session in flat, calm water but then the wind kicks up creating waves. How are you going to adapt? In training for a SUP race, I would often find that my mind would wander and I would be so relaxed that I forgot that I was training. In stand-up paddleboarding, you are dealing with a lot of moving parts- mainly the changing water and weather conditions- and you have to pay attention. However, this is also why paddleboarding is so great, because it forces you to be in the present.

Four O Four (404) performance SUPs: I know that dozens of SUP companies exist and that SUP construction is evolving at an alarming pace, so I don't like to call out specific manufacturers. But since I started training on a 404 this summer I've noticed a world of difference between these carbon fiber constructed boards and the standard rental boards we have at the paddle shop in Lake Tahoe. Even the shape makes a difference...I took out two 404 boards that were the same length, width, and made of the same materials, but I definitely noticed a change in stability just in the shape. As you get more into paddleboarding, you start to notice small things in your equipment and that's why it's best to try out various boards to find the one that's right for you.

Freebird Stand Up Paddleboard Co., Thailand: (**Tip #51**) **If you're into travelling and find yourself at Railay Beach, Thailand (where a James Bond movie was filmed) then you have to check out Freebird Stand Up Paddleboard Co.** While on vacation and looking for a unique adventure,

I joined a Sunset Starlight Night Tour that left at dusk and took you around to the other side of the island in a spectacular 3-hour tour. Our tour was led by the Freebird owner and Thai native a guy named Mann who also works as a tour guide on Railay Beach during the day. With LED lights strapped to our boards, we were able to see fish swimming in the coral beneath us and even saw a baby shark. When we got out to deeper water and it got dark, we tucked in under some cave-like overhangs, shut our paddleboard lights off, and went swimming. As we moved in the water, green glitter sparkled around us- the bioluminescence. It was an incredible experience and enough of a reason alone to visit this part of Thailand. For more information about Freebird, visit www.gofreebird.com.

Full Body Workout: One of the reasons why stand-up paddleboarding is so popular is because it gives you a low-impact, full body workout that helps develop strength, balance, and agility. If you paddle long enough then you'll start to see results and changes in your physique, energy levels, and overall wellbeing. Plus, being on the water in a natural environment is relaxing yet forces you to be in the present and work certain muscles since you are constantly trying to stay on top of an uneven surface.

Fun: **(Tip #52) The main goal of paddleboarding whether you are practicing yoga, entering a race, or just trying to get from point A to point B is to have FUN.** Sometimes when I'm in the midst of a race, dripping in sweat, and fatigue starts to set in, I have to remind myself that I am having fun and that I'm going to feel so good after the race. Then I finish and everyone's cheering and I get this huge sense of accomplishment for even following through and it makes it all worth it despite being sweaty and tired. I love the feeling of how my body reacts after getting a good workout in. So no matter what you're doing on your SUP, pat yourself on the back for taking the time to give your busy life a break by getting out on the water.

Goals, Heart-Healthy Fats, Inflatables

G- Gliding, GPS, Goofy Foot, Grip, Goals, GoPro

Gliding: Gliding on a paddleboard is one of the best feelings in the world because it's like walking on water. Good equipment can play a big part in your ability to glide...for instance, older SUPs can have drag in so that when you stop paddling, the board stops too. However, with certain performance boards, if you stop paddling then the board keeps gliding forward. Those are the best types of boards to use in a race, something that enhances your performance and allows you to put in less work.

Goals: Setting realistic goals is one of the most important steps in training for a SUP race or trying to lose weight, but lots of people get into stand-up paddleboarding for different reasons. **(Tip #53) If your intent is to lose weight with paddleboarding, then I suggest changing your routine where you can implement more**

paddleboarding into your life. I got into paddleboarding because I wanted to become more fit, so I set a goal that I was going to enter a 3-mile race. Therefore, I talked to coaches about what I should eat, how much time I had to dedicate to being on the water to be the most successful, and what I should do on days when the water conditions were too rough. For every race I've set a different goal and then worked towards reaching it. And personally, I always have to have my next race on the horizon to train for otherwise I get lazy and don't practice. Talking to experts and fitness trainers, practicing on the water as often as you can, eating well, and reading my first HowExpert book, *Stand Up Paddle Board Racing For Beginners*, all can offer great advice for how to set goals that are right for you in SUP.

Goofy Foot: I think this term only applies to SUP when you're in the ocean catching a wave. In surfing, wakeboarding, and snowboarding you always have a lead foot, the one that subconsciously jets forward when someone pushes you. If your right foot comes out front, then you are in a "regular" stance and if your left foot comes out first then you are riding in a "goofy" stance- the one that's more unnatural.

Generally, right-handed people have a regular stance and for left-handed people a goofy stance feels more natural to them, but that is not always the case. For instance, I'm left-handed but I ride a wakeboard, snowboard, and surf in a regular stance. Since both of your feet are equally next to each other standing on a paddleboard (like snow skiing) and you are using your paddle to turn instead of your feet then goofy and regular stance don't apply. Except when you are in the ocean and paddling out to a wave to catch it- then you'll have to choose a dominate foot to ride the wave.

GoPro: GoPros are great for recording any type of activity and they are easily mountable to kayaks, helmets, and the noses of surfboards and SUPs. They are a fun accessory to have in capturing the exciting moments of your next SUP adventure.

GPS: When I started training for a SUP race, I invested in a waterproof Garmin Vivo HR watch that tracks distances and times for stand-up paddleboarding. It is my favorite training tool in helping me gage my pace, heart rate, and most of all, distance. Garmin is known for their GPS tools, which is how it is able to provide accurate results. Even for other sports like golfing, running, or snowboarding, I find that GPS tools are the most efficient in using distance to track progress. **(Tip #54) However, different types of GPS tools are ideal to have on you to keep you from getting lost touring or on an overnight SUP camping trip.** The first time I paddled on the Sacramento River, there were times when I didn't know where I was...I saw certain landmarks but I didn't know how close I was (or how long it would take me) to reach my destination. So I pulled out my waterproof-cased iPhone out of my dry bag and checked out where the blue dot was on my Maps app to see exactly where I was. Having GPS tools are a great accessory not only for training but also for safety.

Grip: Grip is another word for the handle on the paddle that's on the opposite side of the blade. Your top hand is always on the paddle, wrapped around the grip in order to complete your strokes (while your

other hand is on the shaft of the paddle). **(Tip #55)**
It's good to have a grip that's soft and flexible
because you may be "gripping" onto it for a
while depending on where you want to go.
Since the paddle and the paddleboard are your two
most important pieces of equipment, you want them
to be comfortable and perfect for your needs.

H- Handle, Heart-Healthy Fats, Head-On, Hull, Hydration Pack

Handle: In stand-up paddleboarding, the handle
refers to the top of the paddle on the opposite side of
the blade (also called the "grip"). This T-bar like part
of the paddle is usually fist-sized and has a soft rubber
foam material that is comfortable in your hand.
Especially in long distance paddleboard races, the
board you are on and the paddle you are using are the
two most important pieces of equipment that will
either hurt you or help you in a race. Therefore, it's
worth investing in a lightweight yet sturdy paddle
with a comfortable handle and a lightweight yet
durable board that will help you glide through the
water.

Head-On: **(Tip #56) If waves are coming**
towards you, paddle through them head on
with the nose of the board slicing directly
through them. It's when you get sideways and
parallel to a wave that you'll flip. The wave will try to
turn you, but paddle straight through it, and get on
your knees and paddle if you need more stability.

Paddling and keeping momentum actually gives you the most stability in rough water conditions.

Heart-Healthy Fats: <u>Muscle and Fitness magazine published a slideshow</u> about the six fats that you need to consume in order to lose fat (and we're not talking about sausage and fries). <u>(Tip #57)</u> **Implementing heart-healthy fats into your diet can help you sustain energy to get you through your paddle session while also reducing inflammation in your body and improving motor skills.** According to the magazine, the top six fats include: wild-caught fish such as tuna, salmon, and mackerel; coconut oil; olive oil; avocados; organic eggs; and nut butter or nuts. For most athletes, staying hydrated is also extremely important during long distance paddles or races. <u>(Tip #58)</u> **Check out the Nutrition section of Chapter 3 to learn more about the best foods to consume for paddling.**

Hull: The hull of a paddleboard refers to the shape of it and how the body is manufactured. There are two main kinds of hulls in SUP- a displacement hull with a deep-looking pointed nose that helps cut through waves by displacing water on either side (like a ship or a motorboat) and a planing hull that is flat, has a rounded nose, which bounces over the waves. <u>(Tip #59)</u> **Before buying a paddleboard, it's best to try out a few different kinds of boards and hulls to see which one you like better (and keep in mind what you'll be using it for).** For instance, many racers like to ride a board that has a displacement hull while some people like boards with the rounder tips to use for yoga and stability.

Hydration Pack: **(Tip #60) Especially when going out on long distance paddles, you always want to stay hydrated.** I like bringing electrolyte tablets and a filtering system for water. Certain energy drinks or goo packs are easy to carry and great sources for keeping stamina and longevity throughout your paddle session.

I- Inflatables, Inland Lake, Indo Board, iSUP, Iodine Tablets

Indo Board: Indo Boards have been around for a while as a balance training tool. An Indo Board is basically a rounded short wooden board (the size of a skateboard but wider like a skimboard) that you balance on top of a plastic roller. **(Tip #61) This is a great fitness tool to use on-land while you're watching TV or some mindless activity where you can place half your focus on balancing.** These are fun to play around on and help work out certain muscles in your legs that will prepare you for balancing better on a SUP.

Inflatables: Inflatable SUPs are great because they are light, durable, and easy to transport. When deflated, they fold up into a backpack with a pump and barely take up any room in your car. Many of them are made with hardened rubber, polyurethane, PVC, and/or polymer. Inflatable SUPs are great for paddling rivers (because hitting a rock is less likely to damage it), the ocean on flat days, and if you are taking an overseas trip and want to save money and get on the water more easily by bringing your own board. It's a bonus if your inflatable comes with a fin and an easy-to-fold-up paddle.

My mom helping me pump up an inflatable SUP before a river race. She's the best.

Inland Lake: Living near an inland lake and stand-up paddleboarding is ideal for wannabe surfers like me who live eight hours away from the closest ocean. This is one of the most popular types of bodies of water to paddle in because it is less hazardous than paddling in an ocean or river, and a lake is more easily accessible since there are a lot more of them around. If you pay attention, there seems to be ponds and lakes everywhere just waiting to paddle on. I personally got into stand-up paddleboarding at Lake Tahoe, a 22-mile by 12-mile alpine body of water that sits in the Sierra Nevada Mountains between California and

Nevada. Stand-up paddleboarding is gaining popularity there because of its beautiful pristine waters. **(Tip #62) Go stand-up paddleboarding at Lake Tahoe and rent your board from Waterman's Landing.**

Iodine Tablets: Whenever I travel to developing countries, (Tip #63) I always take a first aid kit with me with iodine tablets in case I get into a situation where I need access to clean water. However, iodine tablets can be great to take on long SUP trips as well. Many long distance hikers carry them to sanitize water and make it drinkable and since you are likely going to be in the same kind of terrain on your paddleboard, it's worth bringing some along just in case you get thirsty and need clean water.

iSup: I first saw this term pop up from Tower paddleboards when they started sending me emails on their Adventurer and iRace SUP packages. But I've also seen this term in other places...an iSUP is simply and inflatable stand-up paddleboard.

Chapter 5- Terms from J-O Related to Stand-Up Paddleboarding

Journal, Kaizen, Life Jacket

J- Journaling, Jousting, Jam, Jet Ski

Jam: The Webster's dictionary says that "jam" is a bunch of sugar and boiled fruit to create a thick consistency, but in the SUP world it applies to a bunch people getting together to do the sport they love. For instance, "I'm planning on entering the Waterman's Paddle Jam on July 21st". Like a bunch of musicians getting together and playing an impromptu performance somewhere along the way this term transferred over to sporting events, too.

Jet Ski: Often in big lakes or rivers where there are motorboats and kayaks, you may see a motorized personal watercraft or two ripping around as well. **(Tip #64) If you're out paddleboarding and you see a jet ski coming towards you, I suggest heading close to shore.** There are many laws that state that motorized vessels need to be a certain distance away from shore, so that it where you will be the safest in your non-motorized human-powered craft.

Journaling: **(Tip #65) I'm a big believer in keeping a training journal to see how certain variables affect my performance.** Journaling helps keep me on track and forces me work out even when I don't feel like it. Maybe it's because I'm a writer that journaling comes as second nature to me, but it does help keep me accountable to my own goals.

K- Kaizen, Knowledge, Knees, KT Tape, Knife-Edged Bow

Kaizen: This is the Japanese term for "continual improvement" which I believe can be applied to all aspects of one's life including their career, purpose, activity, and especially stand-up paddleboarding. I'm probably getting too deep here, but I feel like the art of kaizen is in stand-up paddleboarding- there's always an opportunity for continuous improvement.

Knees- **(Tip #66) When you first start out stand-up paddleboarding, it's common to start out paddling on your knees before you get comfortable standing up.** Even in certain paddle sessions when I see a big boat wake come my way and am afraid to lose my balance, I'll get down on my knees and paddle through them to avoid going on the water. In my first river race, I also got down on my knees when I reached rippled water or thought it was shallow and was afraid that my fin would hit the bottom. Like surfing, skateboarding, or snowboarding, I have to remind myself to keep my knees bent standing up on my board, too, because keeping a low center of gravity helps with balance.

Knife-edged bow: I actually just learned about this term through a book by Rob Casey. It is a paddleboard that has a pointy nose and displacement hull. These types of boards are some of my favorite to ride.

Knowledge: I find that stand-up paddleboarding also provides endless knowledge...every time I get out on the water I'm remembering and improving on my technique. Just like any other outdoor sport, each day is different in terms of weather, water conditions, and environment. Plus, with paddleboarding there's always something to learn about the equipment and tips from other paddlers.

KT Tape: Short for "Kinesiology Therapy" tape, this is elastic sports tape that can help reduce pressure to your joints. When wrapping it around your skin in a sensitive area, KT tape helps support the muscle and protect it from further injury. **(For more information about this kind of joint support, refer to the "elastic sports tape" definition in Chapter 4).**

L- Leash, Life Jacket, Lesson, Low-Impact, Left Shoulder Turn, Long Distance, Lifestraw, Lake Tahoe Water Trail, Lip Balm, Loaded Board

Lake Tahoe Water Trail: I paddle on a big alpine blue lake that lies between the beautiful Sierra Nevada Mountains and is fed by melted snowfall. The water is so clear that you can see at least 30 feet down, making the vantage point from a stand-up paddleboard great to find all kinds of things below the surface. There are many small towns scattered around Lake Tahoe and many businesses use the pristine location to promote their goods and services.

Created by the Sierra Business Council, the Lake Tahoe Water Trail touts 72 miles of "pure liquid fun" on a paddleboard or kayak with at least 20 public landings to launch or get out at along the way. One of my goals is to take a 4-7 day trip on a paddleboard along the Lake Tahoe Water Trail and challenge myself to explore the whole lake.

The Lake Tahoe Water Trail sign at Waterman's Landing.

Leash: Many people wear a leash while paddleboarding, one part of it attached to the board and a Velcro strap attached around your ankle. **(Lesson #67) Different areas may have different laws on wearing leashes so it's best to check with your local board shop to see if you need one and what type you should get.** For instance, in Lake Tahoe one must always wear a leash but a US Coast Guard-approved life jacket can stay on the board, not the person. This is in case you fall off your board you have a way to get back to it and get your life jacket.

In a river setting, leashes aren't always required because you don't want it to snag on debris and hold you underwater in a current. However, to paddle on a river, **(Lesson #68) you should always at least wear your life jacket and possibly a breakaway leash that is attached to a life jacket or around the waist** so that the board is easily detachable in a sketchy situation. In an ocean setting, many people wear straight leashes on their surfboards so that if they fall catching a wave the board comfortably stays with the person instead of hurting someone else or floating to shore.

In flatwater, a coiled leash is recommended to create less drag in the water while a straight leash is preferable in the ocean (so that the board doesn't bounce back and hit you or the coil get wrapped up in the fin).

Left Shoulder Turn: I recently learned this term in a paddleboard race when the race organizer described the course. He said, "Go 1.5 miles out and make a left shoulder turn around the buoy, then go straight and make another left shoulder turn around the second one". It totally made sense as to which direction you were supposed to go and how to round the buoys in a course...a left shoulder turn means that you approach the buoy on the right side or straight on and pivot around it, keeping your left shoulder closest to the buoy.

Lesson: **(Tip #69) If you want to try stand-up paddleboarding but aren't totally comfortable with being in the water, then I strongly encourage you to take an Intro to SUP lesson.** Many board shops or trainers in your area offer lessons from experts who want to promote the sport of paddleboarding, so they want to get as many people as they can into it and learning the right way. In any watersport, there's a right way and a wrong way to do it; just winging it can cause you to develop bad habits that can lead to injury. Whether you want to do yoga, learn to race, or simply feel more confident on the water, a local professional can help you reach your goals or at least give you some tips to help you become a better paddler.

Life Jacket: **(Tip #70) Also called a PFD (personal flotation device), you should have a US Coast Guard-approved life jacket on you or your board at all times while paddling in rivers or lakes.** I wear an Onyx Belt Pack Manual Inflatable Life Jacket around my waist when I'm in a lake because it's out of my way and comfortable yet supports me if I were to ever get in trouble (just pull the string and it inflates). However, in whitewater or river conditions you may want to wear an actual life jacket or vest...one that is always there and ready for when you unexpectedly fly off your board. Many touring or all-purpose boards have bungee straps on the front that you can tuck your life jacket into if you don't want to wear it. During the safety meeting of the first river race I entered, the Coast Guard captain immediately started out his speech with, "Your life jacket- wear it, wear it, wear it".

LifeStraw: This is an ingenious invention, and a convenient accessory that I'm going to use while paddleboarding. The LifeStraw is a personal water filtering device that can filter up to 1000 liters of water, removing most parasites and waterborne bacteria. One of the most important things about paddleboarding is staying hydrated, and I've found myself in a couple of different situations where I haven't packed a water and then have been dehydrated during a race or a paddle session. In some situations, I just drank the water straight out of the river or Lake Tahoe but if you are in saltwater or paddling somewhere in a developing nation (or even in a marina where you notice garbage and oil in the water), then you definitely don't want to do that. **(Tip #71) While you don't have to have a LifeStraw to paddle, you do want to be prepared with clean water, coconut water, or some kind of natural, good liquid drink that will replenish your body during a long distance touring session.**

Lip Balm: Since many times you will be out in the sunshine sweating your butt off, it's important to stay hydrated and protect your skin and lips. **(Tip #72) Always wear sunscreen and bring chapstick- it will make you feel more comfortable, fresh, and it usually floats or is easy to recover if it falls in the water.**

Loaded Board: A loaded board includes all of the stuff that you bring for your long distance overnight fishing SUP trip, including food, water, emergency kit, sleeping bag, cooler, and the kitchen sink. (Tip #73) **When considering taking your SUP on a multi-day trip, try to do short distances with all of your stuff first to see how you will manage.**

Long Distance: It's pretty subjective as to what a SUPer considers "long distance" but probably changes as you get more comfortable with paddling. When I first started, I thought that three miles was a ways to go but then as I got better and stronger, three miles became my new normal. Now my next goal will be to paddle six miles in an inland lake and get comfortable with that (or try to go 25 miles downstream in a river). At the end of the season in Lake Tahoe, the Tahoe Cup organizers host what is called the Fall Classic that includes a 22-mile race from one end of the lake to the other. My friend and Waterman's Landing owner Anik Wild says that it takes at least six months to a year (or longer) to train for a race of that size. Her husband Jay has done the 32-mile Molokai, which is one of the oldest and largest SUP races in the world where paddlers race across the Ka'iwi Channel between the Molokai and Oahu Hawaiian islands. If you are wanting to venture outside of your comfort zone, just make sure you are prepared, have had adequate training time in, and remember that you're out there to have fun.

Low-Impact: You may hear that stand-up paddleboarding is a low-impact fitness workout that generates results. This means that it's a sport that is not hard on your body or leading to long-term conditions. When done right, SUP can actually alleviate pre-existing conditions allowing you to strengthen your muscles without creating new problems. I love to run, but as I get older I find that the constant contact of my feet hitting the ground can cause knee and ankle soreness. While paddling can create arm and shoulder soreness, it's a different feeling. It's like my muscles are getting stronger, not that I have to put an ice pack to them.

Momentum, Numb Feet, Ocean

M- Motivation, Music, Momentum, Mood Enhancer, Mindset, Mother Nature

Mindset: A lot of people like to just get out on the water and paddle to have fun, but a lot of people also have motivators or specific reasons for paddling. Some examples are to lose weight, stay in shape, hang out with friends, explore new places, connect with nature, or train for paddleboard races. No matter what your reason is, I find that setting a specific goal and working towards it forces me to get out on the water more and even the windiest, choppiest days on the water are still better than not being on the water at all. So no matter what you do, remember that the number one reason to paddle is to have fun and keep a mindset of being safe, prepared, and grateful for your health and opportunity to participate in this exciting new sport.

Momentum: (Tip #74) SUP Instructor Seth Bloomgarden once said that maintaining

momentum on a SUP is like riding a bicycle- the more you can build the more stable you will be. Of course, building momentum on a SUP all has to do with the paddle stroke and flexibility. Just remember, if you stay loose, relaxed, and maybe keep a little bend in your knees, you'll be able to absorb waves and boat chop quicker and keep your momentum moving forward.

Mood Enhancer: Ask people why they paddleboard and they will probably tell you that it's fun, or a way to get out on the water and be in nature, or that they want to stay in shape. There are dozens of reasons why people paddleboard but one of the reasons I like it is because it allows me to escape to think, feel more balanced, be in the present, and it enhances my mood. **(Lesson #75) According to the <u>Health Benefits of Water</u> website, medical studies are starting to show that the negative ions in water and one's proximity to it (whether it be the ocean, river, lake, rain, or even running a humidifier) can create a calming effect** decreasing symptoms of depression, anxiety, and even alleviate fever and asthma attacks.

Mother Nature: No matter where you stand-up paddleboard, as long as you are in the outdoors then you're at the mercy of Mother Nature. She can definitely affect your time out on the water which is why it's important to keep safety and preparedness at the forefront of every paddle experience. However, she also provides some amazing experiences from watching fish jump a foot away from my board to finding myself paddling with a flock of geese. Since she provides serenity and connectedness, I try to do my part by helping to protect the environment and respecting wildlife.

Motivation: So how do you get motivated to go out and paddle in those windy, volatile weather days? For me, it's preparing for a race. When I make a decision to enter a race, I immediately start formulating a game plan of how I'm going to train, how often I'm going to get out on the water, and all of the other factors involved with being prepared. Maybe you are motivated to lose weight, rehab certain muscles, or simply looking for a reason to become more balanced-SUP can provide the answers to all of that.

Music: I love listening to music when I'm out on the water, I find that it's motivating and keeps me focused. I have a waterproof case around my iPhone and keep it close to my body, but I also want to get a Barnacle speaker and Bluetooth it in (securing my iPhone safely in a dry bag). Even if my music dies it's not the end of the world, though, I love listening to the sounds of nature and being more in tune with my surroundings.

N- Nose, Nutrition, Numb Feet, Negative Ions, Neoprene

Negative Ions: As discussed in the "mood enhancer" definition, negative ions contained in water actually create positive health effects. PranaView Australia calls negative ions "the invisible healer" for its ability to enhance mood and stimulate senses. According to the website, a normal ion count in a serene country environment is 2,000-4,000 negative ions per cubic centimeter. Busy polluted cities can have as little as 100 ions and waterfalls can contain up to 100,000 negative ions. Negative ions are caused literally by the force of nature- the gravity of falling water splits neutral air particles and thus freeing them and creating a negative charge. Examples of too many positive ions are clear through pollution or Seasonal Affective Disorder.

Neoprene: Many people ask whether they should wear a neoprene wetsuit while paddleboarding, and I just think that sounds miserable in flatwater because I sweat too much while paddling. I believe that a wetsuit is best to wear when you are in cold water most of the time, like in the ocean. I do have a wetsuit that I wear surfing during the spring and fall months, but I would never think to wear it paddleboarding. **(Tip #76) I usually wear clothing that dries quickly in case I fall in the water- usually yoga pants, a sports bra, tank top, and a long-sleeved shirt and maybe a beanie or gloves when it's cold.** In the fall or winter, I usually wear neoprene booties that keep my feet warm and provide more grip. For paddlers who are in the water a lot, a neoprene hoodie is worth using as well to keep your head from getting that "ice cream brain freeze" feeling by being in cold water. If you live near bodies of water where it's always cold, it may be worth checking out flexible wetsuits and dry suits...the technology of them is constantly improving over time. Cold water paddler Rob Casey provides an excellent description of what you need in cold water paddling in his book, *Stand Up Paddling: Flatwater to Surf and Rivers.*

Nose: The nose of a stand-up paddleboard refers to the front of the board. The nose of a SUP can be pointed (good for racing) or rounded (good for surfing), flat (good for bouncing over or riding waves) or thick like a displacement hull in combination with a knife-edged bow (cutting through waves). Some SUPs have a carrying handle near the nose of the board to easily pull it out of the water and many boards have bungee straps near the nose to hold backpacks, life jackets, or dry bags.

Numb Feet: Having numb feet is pretty common for beginners, as they tend to grip the board with their toes to maintain balance. **(Tip #77) While this tends to go away with time and practice on the water, there are also some things you can do to keep your feet from going numb,** like physically move your body around on the board, wiggle your toes every once in a while, or shift your weight forward or lean back a bit. **Refer to Chapter 3 for more reasons why numb feet happen and solutions for how to prevent it.**

Nutrition: Nutrition is discussed in length in this book, but eating well helps your time out paddling on the water. Food acts as the fuel to help you keep your energy up as well as keep your mental state intact, aiding in your strength and power. **Visit the "What to Eat Before, During and After Paddleboarding" section in Chapter 3 for more information about nutrition, diet, and their relationship to stand-up paddleboarding.**

O- Ocean, Oar, Outrigger

Ocean: The ocean is a popular place for stand-up paddleboarders and arguably where SUP originated. Centuries ago, warriors used to use ancient versions of stand-up paddleboards and paddles to travel from island to island. In recent years, professional surfers found SUP as an activity to keep them out in the water when the ocean was flat, or be able to see good waves from a farther distance and better prepare for catching them. Some pro surfers such as Laird Hamilton and Rob Casey are pioneers in reenergizing the sport, and the evolution took off from there...giving us all flatlanders a way to enjoy the water and stay fit. There are definitely different shapes to SUPs that are more ideal for ocean wave surfing than flatwater though- **(Tip #78) it's best to check your local board shop to see what kind of board is most appropriate for the conditions that you'll be using it in.**

Oar: I've been asked what the difference is between an oar and a paddle, so I looked it up. Apparently, an oar is used for rowing while a paddle is used for paddling. Paddles are used to steer the vessel in a certain direction whereas an oar is used primarily to move a rowboat or outrigger. The main difference between the two is that a stand-up paddleboarder is facing the same direction in which he is paddling whereas a person in a boat is rowing in the opposite direction from which they are facing. I've seen the words "paddle" and "oar" used interchangeably when talking about stand-up paddleboarding, though.

Outrigger: Following up on the differences between an oar and a paddle is the meaning of what an outrigger is. Many traditional SUP races aren't limited to just one kind of human-powered watersport, they can include kayaks, canoes, and outriggers. An outrigger is a modern-day Hawaiian sailing canoe, named for the extra floatable rigging off to the side of the seated area to provide additional stability. One-man and six-man outriggers are common to see in the paddling world and its people use an oar attached to a rowlock to move the vessel around.

Chapter 6- Terms from P-Z Related to Stand-Up Paddleboarding

Paddle, Quickblade, Rest Days

P- PFD, Prone Paddleboarding, Power Phase, Planing Hull, Plan, Paddle, Pump, Paddleguru.com, Protein, Posture, Practice, Paddler's Box

Paddle: I'm sure you've figured out what a paddle is by now and why it is an integral part of stand-up paddleboarding. My friend Jay, an elite paddler, says that **(Lesson #79) your paddle is just as important as your board** and that's why you want to invest in a decent paddle for the type of SUP activity you mostly participate in. For instance, if you are into racing then you want a paddle with a smaller blade that is lightweight and easily catches in the water. If you are catching waves with your SUP, then you may want a paddle that has a wide face on it that helps you stay balanced as you ride the wave.

Paddleguru.com: **(Tip #80) This website is a great resource for paddlers to find out about SUP races going on their area but it's also nice for race organizers because it provides them with timing equipment and extra promotion for their SUP event.** I used paddleguru.com to find out about the first race I entered, Mike's Sunday Fun Race Series in Alameda, California. Between paddleguru.com, the World Paddle Association,

Facebook, and basic Google searches, it's easy to find out about SUP events going on in my area.

Paddler's Box: **(Tip #81) To figure out the placement of where your hands should be on the paddle, hold it up above your head with one hand on the handle and the other at a 90-degree angle.** Wherever that second hand is placed is where it should be when you are paddling. This is called the paddler's box.

PFD: Used as an acronym for "personal flotation device", a US Coast Guard-approved life jacket or PFD is required to have on SUPs in most states in the US. Wearing a PFD or at least having one nearby and accessible while paddling is the best way to save your life in an emergency situation. There are different types of PFDs that are used for different types of paddling. For instance, the waist vest is popular to use in flatwater paddling while a wearable life jacket should be worn at all times in rivers or whitewater conditions. Especially if you are paddling by yourself, always wear your PFD or have it in an accessible place on your board in flatwater conditions and always let someone know where you are going.

Plan: The best way to see results in acquiring better physique and strength is to create a goal on where you want to take your paddleboarding. And then make a plan. If you are training for a race, then finding a coach or a support group to help you with it is key. For instance, I created a goal to enter my first 3-mile SUP race last year, then talked to my friends and created a structure for how I was going to reach it. However, it's also good to be prepared and make a plan for river paddling. Check the currents, read topography maps, and do your research to avoid a sketchy situation (you should do the same thing for oceans and reading tides/changing water conditions).

Planing Hull: Stand-up paddleboards are generally constructed two different ways- one has a displacement hull which cuts through waves by displacing water to either side as it moves through the water. Or a board has a planing hull, a flat bottom and sometimes rounded nose that rides on top of the waves. Planing hull SUP boards are generally wider and more stable, used for yoga, touring, and surfing.

Posture: In stand-up paddleboarding you have no choice but to work on your balance, therefore the effort of SUP is forcing you to practice good posture otherwise you'll fall off your board. Discover Good Nutrition says that stand-up paddleboarding is the best vacation activity ever because it helps you stay fit while enjoying your time off. When you're out paddling, if you are aiming to stay out of the water and on your board as much as possible then you'll be much more aware of your body positioning.

Power Phase: In its Quickblade Paddling Tips: Volume One, Quickblade defines the four phases of the paddle stroke which include the Catch, Power Phase, Exit, and Recovery. **(Lesson #82) In the power phase, a paddler uses their upper body, shoulders, and arms to drive the completely submerged blade through the water.** SUP'ers should finish the stroke and start the Exit phase at their feet; pulling back too far will cause deceleration and inhibit your momentum.

Practice: The only way to get better at paddleboarding is to get on the water and practice, practice, practice. With each session, you will start to get stronger, fitter, and enjoy the sport more. If you need a little help to get motivated, find a support group or a coach at your local paddle shop. I love paddleboarding because it's a constant learning experience that offers many opportunities to push your limits.

Prone Paddleboarding: When I first started working at Waterman's Landing, I had no idea what prone paddleboarding was but then I saw people doing it out in the water and in races. While not as common as SUP, prone paddleboarding is a lot like surfing in the sense that you are laying belly down on your board and using your hands to move through the water instead of a paddle. While SUP tends to be more popular with a general crowd, some prone paddlers state that they feel like they have more of a connection to the water on a traditional paddleboard. Although, you can't see as much going on underneath the water's surface as you can standing up on a board.

Protein: Protein is a group of organic compounds that all living things need to survive. Primarily composed of amino acids, the structural components of protein are found in hair, muscles, enzymes, collagen, and antibodies. According to SUPGlobal Sport Scientist Johanna Shiu, protein makes up about 15 percent of a person's bodyweight mainly stored in the muscles. Especially in long-distance treks, when carbohydrates in the body break down then the protein stored will kick into gear to get you through your paddle session. Hardcore athletes tend to consume more protein than others because they are constantly training and pushing their limits, but fortunately energy drinks and foods high in amino acids are easily accessible to everyone. Some excellent sources of protein include yogurt, fish, meat, cottage cheese, quinoa, milk, and whey.

Pump: When shopping for an inflatable paddleboard, many people wonder how easy it is or how long it takes to pump it up. While pumping up an iSUP can maybe get a little tiring, it's not worth skimping on the air pressure to get on the water faster. Most SUPs come with a standard foot pump which has a gauge that tells you where the PSI (pounds per square inch) should be at. I like to spend the extra time on getting an inflatable SUP to take on a more rigid form, as I find that a board that isn't as pressurized is more wobbly and less stable. While the foot pumps are more commonly used to blow up iSUPs, there are better pumps coming out on the market as well including the <u>K-Pump (that packs down tighter in a bag and doesn't have a handle or a hose to deal with)</u> as well as the <u>Titan Pump</u>, a double-barreled chamber system that pumps up the board in half the time it normally takes.

Here I am pumping up an iSUP in preparation for my first river race.

Q- Quickblade, Quiver

Quickblade: Quickblade is a company that has been around since 1989 that makes some of the lightest and strongest paddles on the market. Created by competitive SUP racer Jim Terrell, Quickblade paddles were named for the blade's quick catch and clean exit in phase three of the stroke. I've only really used Quickblade carbon fiber paddles, but I can tell you that they are far superior then some of the other paddles I've seen and demoed. My friend Jay says that it's worth investing in a good paddle because the performance of the paddle is just as important as the performance of your board. In the first river race I competed in, I raced my brother and halfway through he broke his cheap aluminum paddle that he bought from Walmart and it was a little challenging for him to finish the race. I've also taken out a heavy plastic paddle that felt like it was 15 pounds. After my session, I had bad shoulder pain for days after. **(Tip #83) So it's worth spending a bit more money on something that's durable, won't cause joint issues, and floats in case you drop it in the water.**

Quiver: A quiver refers to a group of boards, whether that be surfboards, snowboards, skateboards, or paddleboards. Many people who are passionate about certain sports like a variety of boards to do certain activities and with SUPs it's no different.

R- Racing, Rack Pads, Rivers, Release, Routine, Rehabilitation, Rest Days, Remount, Right Shoulder Turn, Rails, Recovery Stroke, Relaxing

Racing: As stand-up paddleboarding gains popularity, so is the race scene. Every year I see more and more races popping up on Paddleguru.com and Facebook. They are held on rivers, in oceans, bays, and many on inland lakes and ponds. Many races are structured in distances- on Lake Tahoe there are several races that are 3-mile, 6-mile, and even a 22-mile race at the end of the summer season. However, there are also some other race formats starting to pop up, like the SUPcross on a closed-circuit track (for more information on that, visit prowatercross.com). SUP racing is a great way to challenge yourself and be around other people who are passionate about the sport of SUP. **(Tip #84) Want to learn more about paddleboard racing? Read my first HowExpert book, *Stand Up Paddle Board Racing for Beginners: A Quick Guide on Training for Your First Stand Up Paddleboarding Competition.***

Rack Pads: Many people transport their stand-up paddleboards on the top of their cars like surfboards and fortunately lots of small and medium-sized Sport Utility Vehicles have built in roof racks to strap toys on top. However, placing a SUP directly on one of these racks may cause damage to the board, therefore many paddle shops carry rack pads. Rack pads can help protect the board from the car and keep it safely out of the way while you are driving. Just be sure to get some sturdy rack straps to keep it secured.

Rails: Rails is a term that refers to the sides of a stand-up paddleboard. The shape and construction of your SUP rails can make a huge difference in your performance and the way it connects to the water. The rails affect the drag, grip, and release the board has to the water and determines how much control you have when maneuvering and gaining momentum on the water. SUP designs come with hard rails, rounded rails, and even 60/40 rails which is a combination of a hard and soft rail. For a more in-depth analysis of SUP rails, check out SUPBoarder magazine's article "The Magic of Rails".

Recovery Stroke: According to the Quickblade paddle guide, the Recovery is the last phase of the paddle stroke after the Exit when you return the blade back to the starting point. **(Lesson #85) In the recovery, feather the paddle towards the front of the board and remember to relax your shoulders.** A nice smooth relaxed recovery is the best way to prepare for your next stroke.

Relaxing: I include this term in the glossary because it is a common feeling for how paddleboarding makes one feel...people say that being out in the water and connecting with nature brings on a feeling of being more balanced, rejuvenated, and relaxed.

Release: I've heard this term associated to the third phase of the Quickblade paddle stroke guide when the blade comes out of the water (and it also is correlated to SUP leashes). When paddling in rivers, paddleboarders should always wear a breakaway leash that quickly releases you from the board to avoid being tethered or trapped under the water. However, in oceans or inland lakes a straight or coiled leash is required to wear at all times so you don't lose your board when you fall in the water.

Remount: Getting bucked off of your SUP is inevitable and your ability to remount your board all depends on your physical strength and how comfortable you are in the water. **(Tip #86) If you fall off your board, then I find it's easiest to put the paddle back on it then hoist yourself up to the middle of the board and regain your balance on your knees or sitting down.** Depending on how often you go paddleboarding eventually it becomes second nature to get back on...I remember paddling down the river I got caught in some whitewater and fell off my board but was back on it within three seconds. My brother came up to me in his raft and asked, "Did you fall off your board?" "No," I replied, even though I was soaking wet and missing my sunglasses.

Rest Days: Getting into stand-up paddleboarding is great, but you should pay attention to what your body needs and remember to take some rest days. **(Tip #87)** **If you are training for a paddleboard race or any other type of athletic competition, then taking some time to rest your muscles and store up your energy** will keep you from overtaxing your body that could lead to long-term injury. I know paddleboarding is fun, but switch up your routine every so often and give your body a break when it needs it.

Right Shoulder Turn: I first heard this term in a riders meeting before a paddleboard race as an explanation of how a SUPer should turn around the buoys. A right shoulder turn is where a paddleboarder approaches the buoy from the left hand side and turns with the right shoulder closest to the buoy.

River Paddling: Stand-up paddleboarding in a river is completely different from being in an inland lake or an ocean because now you're dealing with currents, debris, and possibly whitewater and cobble. Paddling in a river is really fun when you're going downstream or dropping into pools, but this kind of paddling does require different accessories and equipment. For instance, I feel more comfortable riding an inflatable SUP in the river in case it hits anything in a moving current and I like using a standard life jacket with a breakaway leash when necessary.

Routine: When training for a SUP race, it's good to set a routine or have some kind of fitness plan leading up to the race. I find that it's good to set a goal and then work with a trainer or a coach to figure out how to reach it. For instance, when planning to enter my first SUP race, I decided to start training four weeks out, dedicating at least four days a week to on-water training. I started paying closer attention to my diet and how certain foods affected my performance in my paddle sessions. A specific training routine isn't necessary for the casual paddleboarder, but if your goal is to lose weight or do well in a race then I think getting a routine in place is important.

Stamina, Training, U-Turns, Vents

S- Strokes, SUP, Strength, Safety, Support, Stamina, Session, Stress Reducer, Surfing, Sweep, SUPcross, Swimming, Shoulder, Shaft, Sunscreen

Safety: **(Lesson #88) Safety should be at the forefront of every paddling session since you are constantly dealing with unknown factors in weather and being exposed to the elements.** You should always make sure you have the equipment you need to safely paddle- always make sure you have a life jacket and leash along with your paddle and board. **(Tip #89) For long distance excursions, bring snacks, hydrating liquids, a VHF radio or working cellphone, whistle, and other safety supplies.**

Session: A session refers to a block of time you spend out in the water paddleboarding, whether that be 15 minutes or three hours. I use this term a lot when training for a SUP competition, breaking down my on-water paddling experiences into "sessions" in appropriately allotted times to help me reach my goals in the race.

Shaft: The shaft is the long part of the paddle where you place your lower hand (while your upper hand is on the handle) to help you move through the water.

Shoulder Injuries: SUP is like any other sport in that if you do it often enough, it may come with injuries. While SUP is a great low impact, full body workout that can relieve pain in other areas, one of the most common injuries in SUP is in the shoulders. The shoulder muscle systems in our bodies are complex in that we are dependent on it for mobility and range of motion. Paddleboarding takes a good amount of using the shoulder blades and ball and socket joints to push through the water. Your rhythm and movement with these joints plays a huge factor in preventing injury and there are some things you can do to keep from getting hurt. For instance, SUPBoarder magazine recommends that **(Tip #90) making sure your paddle is at the right length, working on shoulder stability exercise in a gym, and keeping proper form when you experience fatigue are all ways to keep your shoulders healthy and intact.**

Smile: **(Tip #91) No matter how tough your session is out on the water, remember to smile.** The whole point of paddleboarding is to have fun, so even if you're hot and sweaty and the wind has kicked up and conditions have become challenging, power through it and pat yourself on the back later.

Stamina: There are many types of training plans for building stamina on a SUP, which definitely helps strengthen your muscle mass and improve your overall longevity in any athletic activity you participate in. Wakooda published a beneficial article about **(Tip #92) water exercises you can do to increase your stamina for SUP, including walking or jumping in the water to create resistance and the "trimming your waist" move to strengthen your core.**

Strength: Stand-up paddleboarding is a great way to build up muscle strength because you are constantly trying to balance on an uneven surface while also trying to paddle through the water and gain momentum. Through these activities, you are working your core and abdominal muscles, legs and feet to balance, and arm and shoulder muscles to paddle (and all of it when you fall off your board and have to get back on).

Stroke: The act of moving through the water on a stand-up paddleboard is all due to the power of your paddle stroke. Refer to **Quickblade's Four Phase Paddle Tips guide** to learn about all parts of the stroke and how to perfect your paddling technique to get better and reduce the risk of injury.

Stress Reducer: Stand-up paddleboarding is a great stress reducer because it gets you away from everything going on over on the mainland and allows you to quiet your mind, be in the present, and connect with nature.

Sunscreen: (Tip #93) Since most paddleboarders like to paddle in water when it's warm and sunny outside, sunscreen should be one of the mandatory accessories you take out paddleboarding. Soaking up that vitamin D is great, but make sure your skin is protected. While you're at it, throw on some lip balm too.

SUP: I'm hoping that this term is self-explanatory by now, but just in case you need an exact definition then here it is- SUP is simply an acronym for Stand-Up Paddleboard.

Surfing: Stand-up paddleboarding first originated in the surfing world and was primarily done in oceans before gaining popularity in inland lakes and rivers in recent years. Surfers found that stand-up paddleboarding gave them a better vantage point for catching waves and a paddle could help them move quicker through the water. It also became a way to enjoy the ocean when it was flat and there were no waves, and it's easy to enjoy with young kids or a dog due to the larger size of the board.

Sweep: A sweep is a type of paddle stroke where you jut your paddle out wide and make a half-circle, C motion as you bring it towards your body in the catch. This type of stroke allows your board to turn in a specific direction.

Swimming: Being a strong swimmer or enjoying being in the water is a necessary for stand-up paddleboarding because it's inevitable that at some point you're probably going to fall in. There are all sorts of water exercises you can do to also help you become more comfortable in the water and thus become stronger at paddleboarding.

T- Training, Technique, Turning, Touring, Tail, Throat, Tracking, Trifecta Paddle, Tip

Tail: The tail of a paddleboard refers to the end of it as opposed to the front of it where the nose is. There are a few different shapes that a SUP tail can have, including a rounded shape, pointed shape, or swallow tail shape. Normally 1-3 fins are placed underneath the tail of the board to help you track and glide through the water.

Technique: When getting into stand-up paddleboarding, it's a good idea to **(Tip #93) take a clinic or a lesson and learn proper technique early on so that you don't develop bad habits** that can lead to injury. I've noticed many times when newbies get on the water that their paddle is faced the wrong way or they don't have a leash on. It's best to work with an expert or a pro to learn the correct technique and equipment you should have so that you don't get yourself in a dangerous situation or create unnecessary joint pain down the line.

Throat: The throat of the paddle is the part that is just above the blade. The throat is what attaches the shaft to the blade and should be fully submerged during the power phase of the stroke.

Tip: The tip of the paddle is at the very bottom of the blade, opposite side of the handle.

Touring: There are several different kinds of SUPs on the market that can be used to paddle rivers, do yoga, or race but many people just want to have a board to go out and explore in. A touring board usually is stable and long enough to stash a day's worth of snacks, drinks, and accessories on the bow or back of the board. Touring SUPs come in hard form or inflatables and are a great type to add to your quiver.

Tracking: A SUP's construction, design, and shape all determine how it will track in the water. The type of hull determines what the board does when it comes in contact with waves or rough patches, while the rail shape helps with stability and performance. The shape and size of the fins on your board probably plays the biggest role in tracking and turning, as well as the shape of the tail end of your paddleboard.

Training: When training for a SUP race, it's best to first talk to a coach or expert at your local paddle shop to help you get a plan in place. Many people think that stand-up paddleboarding is easier than it actually is...when I first started I thought that a 3-mile race would be no problem but quickly found that the distances appear closer than they actually are. You need to build up your upper body strength in order to not experience fatigue or wear out. We all naturally learn to walk pretty early on in life and practice it pretty often, but with paddling you have to work on building up arm and shoulder muscle since it's not as natural.

Trifecta Paddle: Not all paddles are made the same and the quality of the construction can make a drastic difference in your performance. Recently Quickblade came up with a paddle called the Trifecta that contains a good balance of flex and stiffness that is ideal for touring, racing, and surfing. (Lesson #94)

A hybrid paddle is also more forgiving on the wrists and shoulders.

Turning: Trying to change directions on your SUP definitely takes practice, but is an essential part in all kinds of paddleboarding (especially in the ocean when you're trying to catch waves and need to pivot your board in time to grab them). There are always different turns that you can practice and get better at like pivoting, the C-sweep, the crossbow, pivot, and poke.

U- Upright, U-Turns, Upstream

Upstream: (Tip #95) I've heard that a good way to train for a SUP race is to work on paddling in different water conditions and paddling upstream. In college, when my friends wanted to build their strength up for a month-long surf trip, they took their boards to the river and paddled up stream. The same can be done for preparing for a stand-up paddleboard trip. Just know how to read the river before you go out and make sure you pick a spot with a current that you can safely handle.

Upright: Being upright on a SUP is the difference between stand-up paddleboarding and a regular prone paddleboard. Stand-up paddleboarding helps with posture and developing core strength.

U-Turn: Doing a U-turn around a buoy or back to the shore on a SUP is something that doesn't come easily despite how natural professional paddleboarders make it look in races and competitions. The most efficient way to do a U-turn on a SUP is to back your body up on the board so that the nose is sticking up higher and the weight distribution matched with the paddle stroke will help you whip the board around. However, this is an advanced move and takes a lot of practice to get comfortable moving your body around on the paddleboard.

V- Vents, Variable Weather, Vitamin D, Videos, Vest, V-Drive Paddle, VHF radio

Variable Weather: The thing with stand-up paddleboarding is that being on water forces you to interact with a natural environment and since most of the time SUP is done outdoors, there can be variable weather. **(Tip #96) I always check the weather conditions and water temperatures before going out and make sure that I'm prepared with the appropriate clothing and equipment I need.** Even when Lake Tahoe looks gorgeous and calm I know that the wind can kick up and conditions can change fast, therefore I always check Windfinder to try to get an idea of what the weather is going to do. The key to having fun on a SUP is to be safe and be prepared, so always have an idea of what kind of waters- and weather- you're getting into.

Vents: Many stand-up paddleboards have either a handle or a vent in the middle of the board that make it easy to transport to and from the water. **(Tip #97) The vent of the SUP also gives a good**

indication of where your feet should be placed on the board since it's normally right in the middle of it to make it easier for carrying.

Vessel: Many SUPs are referred to as human-powered floating vessels and some areas require special permits to take a SUP (or a human-powered vessel) on certain waterways.

Vest: A Coast Guard-approved life vest should always be worn in rivers and inland lakes and can be the difference between life and death in an emergency situation. Safety should always be on the forefront of your paddling experiences.

VHF radio: While going on long SUP excursions or touring open waters, it's a good idea to have both your powered-up cell phone and a marine VHF radio on you. A VHF radio is generally installed on all ships and even smaller seafaring watercraft, used to communicate with other captains and call in emergency situations. Fortunately, they make handheld waterproof radios that can fit in a life jacket or on your board. **(Tip #98) A VHF radio is a great thing to have to communicate with fellow mariners when paddling on an open waterway.**

Videos: I like to watch paddleboarding videos while training for a race and hopefully pick up some techniques and tricks from the pros. The Red Bull channel is a great resource for all watersports-related material because they always find the pros that are pushing the limits in athletic ability. YouTube is also a great source for short How To videos.

Vitamin D: Another reason why stand-up paddleboarding is so fun is because many people do it on nice warm days when there's plenty of sunshine giving you lots of vitamin D. Paddling on water also gives you a quick and easy way to cool off if you get too much sun. Just make sure you wear lots of sunscreen and stay hydrated.

V-Drive Paddle: Another one of Quickblade's inventions, the V-Drive is also a performance paddle that is ideal for catching waves, touring, and racing. A unique V-scoop is the basis of its design, creating dihedral edges for enhanced stability and effortless glide.

Whitecaps, XD, Yoga, Zen

W- Waves, Water, Weather, Wind, Wetsuit, Whistle, Windfinder.com, Whitecaps, Waist Vest

Waist Vest: When I first started paddleboarding I started seeing all of these people out on the water with these fanny packs around their waist, but they never put anything important in them like their keys or cell phone. I eventually learned that these were manually inflatable life jackets/PFD's that go around the waist, allowing for more maneuverability while paddling. **(Lesson #99) When you fall off your board or need to use it, you pull the tab that hangs out the front which releases CO2** and causes it to inflate (then reload it or replace the cartridge after use). When I first started paddleboarding, I wore a regular life jacket but found that I got too hot. I recently bought a waist vest and I love it because it's so out of the way yet provides the support I need.

Water: Water is the basis where all paddleboarding occurs, whether it be on a lake, ocean, bay, river, or indoor swimming pool. Water has incredible healing benefits and medicinal properties, making a great place to enjoy the exciting new sport of stand-up paddleboarding.

Waves: Encountering waves on a SUP is an inevitable part of the sport if you do it often enough, especially in the ocean or on a big inland lake where the weather is constantly changing (like where I live in Lake Tahoe). **(Tip #100) Check out Windfinder before you go out to see what the wind is going to do that day and gage what you are comfortable paddling in.**

Weather: Weather plays an important role in your paddleboarding experience. Up in Lake Tahoe, we have four distinct seasons and even in the warm summer months the weather is changing all the time. Always check the weather conditions before going out on your favorite waterway and make sure you are as prepared as you can be for what lies ahead.

Wetsuit: People always ask if I wear a wetsuit while paddleboarding and the short answer is, "no". I mainly paddle on an inland lake and while the water is cold, I try to stay out of it most of the time. When I'm paddling hard, I get hot and sweaty and being in a wetsuit just sounds miserable. I like to wear breathable clothing that's not too loose yet not too tight and dries fast when I fall in the water. However, if you are paddling in a place where you're in cold water most of the time (like the ocean) then you may want to wear a wetsuit and neoprene hoodie and booties to stay warm.

Whistle: When I first started paddleboarding, I noticed that on the standard rental boards I went out on that a bright orange PFD was attached to the board along with a whistle. (Tip #101) **This small, light instrument comes in quite handy in an emergency situation and is good to have on any paddle trip (especially if you're going out by yourself).**

Whitecaps: Whitecaps are caused when there's rough water and the waves get so big that they start curling over and appearing "white" at the crest. Generally whitecaps occur in waters where wind is whipping through at 15 mph winds or higher, making it too rough to go out paddleboarding unless you are an expert. In Lake Tahoe, you can watch the wind come in when the water gets darker and then it's best to double-check the weather or start getting back to shore.

Wind: Wind definitely plays a role in how much fun you'll have on the water. Wind can blow in at any time whether you're paddling on a river, lake, or ocean and affect how far you can go, your balance, and stability on the board. When training for a race, I would go out on Lake Tahoe on semi windy days and just paddle against the waves (it was like being on a treadmill). However, I do not suggest that beginners go out in rough water as it can be hard to stay on the board and you may get yourself in a scary situation.

Windfinder: Windfinder is a website/smartphone applications that gives 7-day forecasts on wind conditions in many bodies of water. Just like surfers depend on special watches that check the tidal waves on oceans, **(BONUS Tip #102) Windfinder is the best source to check the wind conditions for paddleboarders.** It provides a pretty accurate hourly forecast of air temperatures, weather, wind direction, winds gaged in mile per hour speeds, and max gusts. I check this app every time I think about going out paddleboarding. NOAA is a good resource as well for all things weather-related.

X- XD, X factor, XTerra

XD: There are very little words in general that begin with X, let alone ones related to paddleboarding. Therefore, I wanted to share this squinty-eyed laughing emoji instead. Studies show that the negative ions in the water cause happiness, which is probably why the combination of getting a great workout in while being on the water makes paddleboarders feel like squinty-eyed laughing emoji's (especially when enjoying it with friends).

X factor: An X factor refers to something that's a special talent, above and beyond what average people can do, something that sets them apart. I include this term because sometimes I'll watch a SUP race, or a video where a waterman or woman just has this special ability that puts them above the rest. Professional athletes in the top 10 percent of their field are able to get there with lots of practice, training, and approaching their craft with the right mindset.

XTerra: XTerra is a company that specializes in wetsuits, speedsuits, and inflatable SUPs. They also sell accessories including paddleboard pumps, swim gloves, dry bags, and neoprene SUP pants.

Y- Yoga SUP, Yonder

Yoga SUP: Yoga has been around for centuries and has helped millions of people get fit, find balance, and improve their mindset and overall wellbeing. Stand-up paddleboarding does the same thing, so it makes sense for a movement to be in place to combine the two. I remember going to my friend's yoga studio in Costa Rica in 2012 and we took a day to take the SUP out in a bay. I watched her do a headstand on her board and was blown away. There are even specifically-designed SUPs made specifically for yoga; they are stable, wide and have soft foam tops for when you fall off practicing that headstand.

Yonder: I've always known the term "yonder" to mean discovering what's beyond what you don't know, taking a chance and paddling around the corner, seeing what's on the other side. Yonder is also a smartphone app that connects people with each other and use community knowledge to find new places to hike, camp, paddle, and enjoy the outdoors.

Z- Zen, Zone

Zen: It's pretty common for stand-up paddleboarding to put a person in a state of Zen; being out in nature can give the feeling of peace and meditative calmness by being in the present and aware of your surroundings. The Urban Dictionary suggests that Zen is a state of mind that includes being totally focused and body working in harmony with itself.

Zone: When training or entering a SUP race, it is pretty common to get "in the zone"- the place where you are at your peak performance. Your heart rate is up, you are going your fastest and feel your best. I use a GPS-enabled waterproof watch to track my sessions and see when I paddled the hardest, when I leveled off, and how I need to improve the next time.

Well, these are all of the terms I could think of that have to do with stand-up paddleboarding. I hope that you enjoy them and can relate (I even tried to throw in a bonus tip or two). Thank you for reading this glossary of SUP terms and feel free to keep reading about how to train for a SUP race and my 2018 training diary. More about training for a SUP race for beginners can be found in my other HowExpert book.

Chapter 7- Top Four Tips For How to Train For a SUP Race

(Portions of this article were published in the Tahoe Weekly in May 2018)

It is the beginning of May and I'm the only one on Lake Tahoe, cruising on top of the water on a stand-up paddleboard going from Waterman's Landing to Mourelatos and back. I'm equipped with a life jacket, a dry bag, my paddle, and a Garmin Vivo waterproof watch to track distance, time, and heart rate. I'm training for my first 3-mile race of the season, the Tahoe Cup Series Stop #1 which will fortunately be held at my training grounds of Waterman's Landing.

I just started getting into SUP racing last autumn, the tail-end of paddleboarding season in Tahoe. However, I quickly became hooked as I realized what a great place Lake Tahoe is to train in, how stand-up paddleboarding provides a convenient way to enjoy the lake, and I've found great comradery between fellow athletes. So as we get into summer and more SUP races start popping up, here are some tips for how to have a successful paddleboard race:

1. Get a Good Coach (or support group)

Sometimes it's hard to know exactly where to start in training for a SUP race, and a coach can really help guide you in the right direction. Fortunately, my training ground is also home to two world-renowned paddlers- Jay and Anik Wild. As owners of Waterman's Landing (along with Kina Nemeth who runs the café), they have a vested interest in developing athletes/healthy people and growing the sport.

They host clinics and lessons all summer long from an Intro into SUP and swimming cross-training clinics to ongoing weekly SUP yoga clinics and junior waterman camps.

The Wilds offered tips, encouragement, and motivation which not only helped me train, but kept me safe as well. They were not afraid to tell me when it just wasn't worth it to go out or offer insights into my training method. Like one day Jay gently reminded me to paddle directly into the waves that kept me from flipping into the water, or after sharing my time and distance with Anik one morning, she simply told me "good job" which really meant a lot that she paid attention to my progress.

2. Set Realistic Goals

Also, a good coach can help you set realistic goals. When I was training for my first paddleboard race last autumn, I originally set a goal to not come in last. But what would've happened if I was the only one who entered the race? Therefore, I changed it...I wanted to set a new personal record (I ended up doing both- I beat my own time and got third out of six people in the race).

Jay also told me to not beat yourself up when you don't meet your goal, that every competition is a learning experience. But with that being said, you don't want to get in over your head and enter the 22-mile South Shore to North Shore race without being prepared...a good coach helps motivate you, keep you on track, and forces accountability. A trainer can also help you with your diet. Personally, I think that I naturally start eating healthier when I'm training because I feel that diet is directly related to performance. The most physically fit people I know put natural, organic ingredients in their bodies. After a training session, I've found that I crave a gluten free granola bar or vegan pumpkin bread to replenish my body. It seems that the Paleo diet offers the right mix of proteins and carbs to sustain one through a race because that diet is all about getting back to the basics of food. Besides, who wants to eat a donut or processed junk before a big workout (or afterwards)?

3. Start Training Early

Depending on what shape a person is in, one should start training for a SUP race at least four weeks in advance for a 3-6 mile race and at least six months to a year for a long distance race (like the 22-mile South Shore to North Shore Fall Classic). The key is to get out on the water as much as possible to build up strength, balance, and endurance.

So here I am, four weeks out from my first race of the season. The good news is that the weather is sunny on most days, the bad news is that the wind keeps kicking up in the afternoons. While the air temperature is starting to warm up, the water is still in the low 50's (deemed "too cold to swim").

I did not want to fall in. After a day of paddling against a wind so fierce I stayed in one place, Windfinder.com soon became my best friend for planning the most ideal times to train out on the water- which was many times at 7am.

Some days the weather was so crazy that it was impossible to train on the water, so I settled for other exercises instead. I played golf, went running, renewed my gym membership (and used it). It's good to mix up workouts when the lake is too choppy and sometimes you have no other choice. For instance, CrossFit is a great rainy day activity because you have access to varied equipment like pull-up bars, kettlebells, and rowing machines and can help build your muscles for when it's time to paddle. Anik told me that any type of cross-training for any sport is usually helpful. "I'm glad I worked out throughout the winter so I could keep my muscle memory intact for paddling season," she told me.

4. Go In With the Right Mindset

Remember that the whole point of paddle boarding is to have fun, so don't beat yourself up if you don't make the podium on your first race. No matter how much you train, there are always unknown variables like timing, weather, changing water conditions, how the race is organized, et cetera that can affect performance.

For me, just having a race on the horizon gets me out on the water more than I normally would and gives me something to look forward to. Jay once told me to have no expectations- to just go out there and have fun- so I always try to give myself a pat on the back just for showing up and putting in the work to train. Meeting my goals is a bonus.

The key to doing well in a race is to set realistic goals and get out on the water as much as possible.

Chapter 8- My Personal Race Training Diary for the 2018 SUP Season

How I Trained For My First Race of the Season

In late April 2018, the owners at Waterman's Landing in Lake Tahoe announced that they were taking over the Tahoe Cup, a 4-event race series with distance courses ranging from 3 miles to 22 miles. At that time, the snow was melting off the mountains and I was jonesing to get back out on the water again. I decided that I was going to enter the first race of the series, the 3-mile race within the May 26 Memorial Race and that I wanted to do it in 45 minutes. Using my GPS-enabled Garmin Vivo HR waterproof watch, I tracked my progress, recorded it, and eventually reached my goal. Here's a glimpse into my fitness regimen when preparing for a SUP race:

4/20/18: This was my first day back out on the water. I leisurely paddled to Mourelatos Lakeshore Resort and back (4 miles roundtrip) with my cousin. We did it in 3 hours.

4/30/18: I went 1.25 miles to the yellow boathouse off in the distance and back in 5-7 mph waves.

5/3/18: I went a leisurely 3 miles in calm water in 1 hour 13 minutes.

5/9/18: I went half a mile in 16 minutes in whipping winds out towards the boathouse. I could hear the wind racing through my paddle, whistling like a flute.

5/10/18: It's hard for me to be out on the lake by myself without anyone pushing me. On the way out to Mourelatos, I tried to keep up with a tugboat but it quickly pulled away from me going at least 5 miles per hour. I remember trying to catch up with Anik on the water one morning last season, but she was going double the speed I was.

Therefore, I'm learning to trick myself into going faster. On my way back from Mourelatos, I imagined being late for a meeting or tasting the delicious coffee waiting for me in the café. That made me push ahead, thinking that I had somewhere else I needed to be right at that time.

I paddled 4 miles in 1.15 hours, which Anik says is pretty good. It's tough not to have any point of reference (I tried to race that tugboat), but I definitely feel like I'm getting stronger every day.

5/11/18: It was supposed to be another windy day, but I wanted to get one more on-water training session in before the weekend. I wanted to go to the point past the boathouse and back, three miles total. Winds are supposed to kick up to 6-7mph by 8am and according to Windfinder, the lake will be completely blown out by 11am (10-22mph winds throughout the rest of the day).

I get out on the water at 7am and head towards the boathouse. I don't really notice the wind because it's at my back, gradually aiding me along. However, it was hard trying to round the buoy, the wind offering a forceful resistance. I kept pushing/paddling into it trying to keep my board head-on into the waves because that was the only way I could keep my momentum and get anywhere.

The air temp was also about 37 degrees and while I had a beanie and neoprene booties on, I forgot any gloves and my hands went numb.

It started to calm down as I reached the little inlet towards Waterman's Landing and easily coasted in, remembering why I liked paddleboarding so much. But I have to admit that it was the most challenging workout I've ever had. And I only went 2.08 miles in 48 minutes, so far away from my goal (I think I averaged a 24-min. pace). But I'm glad I went out when I did though because by 9:30am the lake was white-capping and I know it would've been too late to train that day.

5/13/18: While out of town, I did a 1-mile run that took about a half-hour.

5/15/18: I did a 2.84-mile paddle in 50 minutes, averaging a 17-minute pace and then ran a 5k in the gym.

5/16/18: I did 150 stairs at the gym instead of going to the lake because it was pouring rain outside (however, the lake was calm). The stair machine helps build endurance and I could definitely feel my heart rate get up there.

5/17- I paddled 2.94 miles in 52 min averaging a 17 minute pace. I'm slowly getting towards reaching my goal.

5/19- I paddled 1 mile in 11.46 minutes and then did a 2-mile bike ride.

5/22- I got on the stair master and did 150 floors in 52 minutes.

5/23- I paddled 3 miles in an hour and 12 minutes, taking my time.

5/24- I paddled 3 miles in 53 minutes and feel like it's time to upgrade to a better board. Went 4.5 miles total, with a 20-minute break.

5/18/18: It took me 36 minutes to go 2.2 miles and I managed a 16.3-minute pace (my fastest ever). The lake was calm and it was sunny; I maintained a steady, confident stride and started shedding layers halfway to Mourelatos. I think that I paddle faster with less clothes on, which is why I can't imagine doing a race in a constricting wetsuit. I took my time on my way back and circled around some bobs attached to fishing lines, accidentally pulling up a crawfish trap. Even taking my time, I managed a 20-minute pace- faster than when I started paddleboarding last fall.

I think what really helped me set a record pace was that I ate breakfast beforehand (gluten free pancakes with blueberries and peanut butter on them). In the last couple of days, I've been training so early (starting at 7-7:30am) that I hadn't eaten anything a lot of the time and couldn't sustain my energy throughout the whole session. Kina also gave me a paleo ball; it was rich and chocked full of protein. One is perfect before and after a paddle session. They are made with coffee flour, coconut oil, cacao, and almond butter.

5/19/18: I biked a mile down to Waterman's Landing, worked until 2pm-ish, and then went out on the water because it was still glass. I paddled about 2 miles in 36 minutes, averaging a 20-minute pace. It wasn't that great- I think it was because I was hopped up on coffee but hadn't eaten anything all day. I need to remember to pop one of those chocolate paleo balls for quick energy when I go out.

5/22/18: Did 150 floors on the stair master at the gym in 51 minutes. I watched the Red Bull channel- Paradigm Lost and Ian Walsh training for a big wave surfing event.

5/25/18: It's a day before the Waterman's Memorial Race and I took out a new carbon fiber 404 demo board. I went 1.85 miles in 35 minutes. I felt a little wobbly at first, but felt more confident as I kept paddling. I love this board- it cuts through the waves and moves forward even when I'm not paddling.

That evening, I went to the Lake Tahoe Watermans Association/pre-registration party fundraiser and ran into a guy I met at the Folsom Lake race last October. I met some other fellow racers and felt a little more comfortable about what was to come the next morning.

5/26/18: RACE DAY

I wake up at 6:30am, the day of the race. It's cloudy and cold, but fortunately not snowing like a lot of Memorial Day Weekends in Lake Tahoe. At 8am, I ride my bike down to Waterman's Landing to check in and get my bib number.

It's not super hectic down there, but there is a bit of activity. I check in, but find that the 404 I used yesterday isn't in its rack. I start to get worried- it's now a half an hour before the race and I don't have a board. I contemplate using one of the NSP Elements, but was so happy with the 404 that I wanted a fast board.

I try out Anik's board, but it was way too small and tippy; I felt like I would've gone flying into the water the second I got too close to someone or encounter a small wave. Thinking I was going to settle with an NSP, Jay pulled through and offered me a brand-new 404 board out of the box for me to use in the race. It was the same size as the one I tried out the day before, but had a different shape.

Minutes before the race started, my friend and co-worker Corey was putting the fin on my board, finding a leash, and helping me secure a life vest. It was a tight start, but I chatted with one of the competitors next to me and it helped calm my nerves.

At least 20 of us were lined up for a dry land start and at the sound of the air horn, we were off. This is where I made my first mistake- I stood up too soon. When I got up, it seemed like the majority of the pack was already 10-20 yards ahead of me.

But it was good because I had a lot of people pushing me in that race, a lot of people on the horizon to try to catch up to. At times I slowed down when I hit boat chop, but overall I felt pretty stable on the board. I definitely felt fatigue before I was even halfway there, though (note to self: train at farther distances). I eventually caught up to my friend Nikki and we were head-to-head for half a second before we reached the buoy. She whipped around it fast and I went wide, headed out towards the middle of the lake rather than the finish line. She pulled ahead and I could never catch up.

Heading towards the big red finish line felt better than going away from it, and Jay was coming by on his Jet Ski to cheer us on. To see everyone waiting on the beach, my boyfriend taking pictures and my friend Jess doing the timing, it was an incredible feeling. And I was exhausted, I definitely felt like I did my very best.

Overall, I got 11th out of 16 men and women in the 12'6" SUP division. Although I didn't do great standings-wise, I met my goal of doing the race in 45 minutes. I felt like I got a crazy good workout in, made some new friends and reconnected with some old, and learned a few things about how to improve my time in the next go-around. And that post-race chicken burrito was one of the best meals I ever had.

I went home, took a nap, and started planning for my next race.

Chapter 9- Additional Resources

Conclusion

Even though I'm pretty new to stand-up paddleboarding, I'm passionate about the sport (or anything that has to do with water). Although I've been wakeboarding for the last 20 years, I like that all you need is a board and a paddle to get out on the water. Writing this book has inspired me to pay closer attention to everything related to SUP and the water, and I hope you have learned something as well.

References to Websites, Shops, and Coaches

With that being said, this book wouldn't have been made possible without the help of the owners at Waterman's Landing. Jay and Anik Wild and Kina Nemeth have offered continual encouragement, support, tips, and advice on how to eat well. If you ever want to take a clinic, class, or sign your kids up for a waterman's camp, check out www.watermanslanding.com.

I also really loved Rob Casey's book, *Stand Up Paddling: Flatwater to Surf and Rivers*. It is a thorough and well-written guide about how to read water conditions, how to prepare for certain paddle sessions, and it includes expert tips from a top pro himself.

I've found paddling communities through Facebook, Google, and Paddleguru.com. The World Paddle Association website is also a good resource for upcoming professional events.

Windfinder, NOAA, and www.americanwhitewater.org are great resources for reading weather, water, and river conditions. Always be prepared with the proper equipment and maps that you need and paddle with a buddy if you can. If you go out by yourself, let someone know where you're going and how long you expect to be gone.

If you've got the basics of stand-up paddleboarding down and are ready to enter a race, then I suggest you find a good coach by visiting your local board shop or Googling SUP trainers in your area. However, if you decide to do it all on your own, at least check out my first HowExpert book titled *Stand Up Paddle Board Racing For Beginners*. It's available to buy on Amazon. Mike's Paddle in Alameda, California, also puts on a really fun beginner race series right there in the San Francisco Bay Area.

Thank you for reading and I hope to see you out on the water soon!

About the Expert

Based in Lake Tahoe, California, Kayla Anderson loves to read, write, and play in the outdoors. In summer 2017, Kayla began working for one of the best paddleboard rental/coffee shops in America called Waterman's Landing. There, she has access to some of the best paddleboards, the water, and advice from two elite paddle board racers. She fell in love with the sport of SUP because it allows her to be out in the water more often than she already is. Kayla also writes for The Tahoe Weekly and Enjoy Northern California Living magazine. This is her second HowExpert book on stand-up paddleboarding.

HowExpert publishes quick 'how to' guides on unique topics by everyday experts. Visit HowExpert.com to learn more.

Recommended Resources

www.HowExpert.com – Quick 'How To' Guides on Unique Topics by Everyday Experts.

www.HowExpert.com/writers - Write About Your #1 Passion/Knowledge/Experience.

www.HowExpert.com/membership - Learn a New 'How To' Topic About Practically Everything Every Week.

www.HowExpert.com/jobs - Check Out HowExpert Jobs.